Cambridge Elements

Elements in the Philosophy of Georg Wilhelm Friedrich Hegel
edited by
Sebastian Stein
Heidelberg University
Joshua Wretzel
Pennsylvania State University

HEGEL'S PHILOSOPHY OF NATURE

Christian Martin
University of Stuttgart

Shaftesbury Road, Cambridge CB2 8EA, United Kingdom

One Liberty Plaza, 20th Floor, New York, NY 10006, USA

477 Williamstown Road, Port Melbourne, VIC 3207, Australia

314–321, 3rd Floor, Plot 3, Splendor Forum, Jasola District Centre, New Delhi – 110025, India

103 Penang Road, #05–06/07, Visioncrest Commercial, Singapore 238467

Cambridge University Press is part of Cambridge University Press & Assessment, a department of the University of Cambridge.

We share the University's mission to contribute to society through the pursuit of education, learning and research at the highest international levels of excellence.

www.cambridge.org
Information on this title: www.cambridge.org/9781009557771

DOI: 10.1017/9781009557757

© Christian Martin 2025

This publication is in copyright. Subject to statutory exception and to the provisions of relevant collective licensing agreements, no reproduction of any part may take place without the written permission of Cambridge University Press & Assessment.

When citing this work, please include a reference to the DOI 10.1017/9781009557757

First published 2025

A catalogue record for this publication is available from the British Library

ISBN 978-1-009-55777-1 Hardback
ISBN 978-1-009-55778-8 Paperback
ISSN 2976-5684 (online)
ISSN 2976-5676 (print)

Cambridge University Press & Assessment has no responsibility for the persistence or accuracy of URLs for external or third-party internet websites referred to in this publication and does not guarantee that any content on such websites is, or will remain, accurate or appropriate.

For EU product safety concerns, contact us at Calle de José Abascal, 56, 1°, 28003 Madrid, Spain, or email eugpsr@cambridge.org

Hegel's Philosophy of Nature

Elements in the Philosophy of Georg Wilhelm Friedrich Hegel

DOI: 10.1017/9781009557757
First published online: November 2025

Christian Martin
University of Stuttgart

Author for correspondence: Christian Martin,
christian.martin@philo.uni-stuttgart.de

Abstract: Recent years have seen new systematic interest in Hegel's philosophical conception of the physical universe. It has become clear that Hegel's account of nature is revealing both on its own and by providing a non-naturalist understanding of the place of mind in nature. This Element focuses on the very foundations and method of Hegel's philosophy of nature, relating them to Newtonian and to modern physics. The Element also sheds light on Hegel's global account of the physical universe as a material space-time system and on his ecological conception of the Earth as a habitable planet populated by organic life. By drawing connections to relativity theory and earth systems science it is shown that Hegel's conception of nature is very much philosophically alive and can complement scientific accounts of nature in illuminating ways.

Keywords: Hegel, nature, philosophy of nature, space and time, matter

© Christian Martin 2025

ISBNs: 9781009557771 (HB), 9781009557788 (PB), 9781009557757 (OC)
ISSNs: 2976-5684 (online), 2976-5676 (print)

Contents

1 Hegel's Philosophy of Nature in Context   1

2 *Mechanics*: Space, Time, Motion, and Heavy Matter   33

    Abbreviations   59

    References   60

1 Hegel's Philosophy of Nature in Context

1.1 Philosophy of Nature and the Scientific Revolution

According to Hegel, philosophy of nature is a "young,"[1] distinctively "modern"[2] discipline. Its background is the scientific revolution and the emancipation of physics from philosophy it brought forth. In light of this emancipation Hegel refers to physics as "former natural philosophy."[3] Hegel provided his own extensive treatment of philosophy of nature in the second volume of his *Encyclopedia of the Philosophical Sciences in Basic Outline* (1817).[4] As he acknowledges, it was Kant who first devised "philosophy of nature" as a philosophical discipline meant to *complement* the scientific approach to nature. How it was supposed to do so is manifest in the title of the work which, according to Hegel,[5] laid the foundation for modern philosophy of nature: *Metaphysical Foundations of Natural Science* (1786). Kant thereby alludes to Newton's *Philosophiae Naturalis Principia Mathematica* (1687) which had inaugurated physics as a self-standing discipline. Mathematized physics, on Kant's accord, requires a philosophical foundation. Even while post-Kantian thinkers such as Schelling and Hegel conceived of the relation between philosophy of nature and natural science in ways that substantially differ from Kant's, all of them understood philosophy of nature as a kind of inquiry into nature which complements natural science without relying on the objective validity of scientific theories or merely reflecting on their methods. Philosophy of nature, in other words, does not amount to philosophy of science, which is a distinctively later achievement.

To understand why Kant and post-Kantian thinkers devised a philosophical inquiry into nature that is meant to complement the modern scientific approach to nature, we need to roughly bring into view what they take to be distinctive of

---

[1] $24.2,957^5$. References to Hegel's works are given by recourse to volume number, page number, and line numbers of *Gesammelte Werke*, the only critical and complete edition available. Acronyms are explained in the section "Abbreviations" at the end of this Element. All English translations are my own. English editions of Hegel's works are referenced in the bibliography.
[2] $24.2,775^{2\text{-}11}$.   [3] $20,236^2$.
[4] Extended and revised editions of the *Encyclopedia* appeared in 1827 and 1830. For an illuminating account of Hegel's idea of a philosophical encyclopedia and the role of the *Encyclopedia* in academic teaching cf. Fulda 2003, 126–133. Many editions of the *Encyclopedia* that were published after Hegel's death contain so-called "additions" which were compiled by Hegel's literary executors from students' notes. GW 24.3 provides a critical edition of these additions whose immediate sources are often difficult to trace. GW 24.1 and GW24.2 render students' transcripts of Hegel's various lectures on the philosophy of nature which were designed to orally elaborate on the "basic outline" provided by the *Encyclopedia*. These transcripts are an indispensable further source beyond the *Encyclopedia* for anyone engaging with Hegel's mature philosophy of nature.
[5] See $20,254^{14\text{-}18}$.

that approach. Science is an exemplary modern achievement in virtue of prioritizing thought over being: While its task is to cognize the physical universe, it does not do so by relying on a realm of natural substances which appear to be there anyway. What science relies on is rather a distinctive kind of method that artificially distinguishes and isolates certain traits of natural phenomena, namely, ones which promise to specifically vary with one another, in order to discover recurrent correlations between them.[6]

Both experiment and mathematization are species of this general type of method which lend themselves to be combined.[7] Experiment differs from mere observation by intervening into natural processes in a way that seeks to isolate features of these so as to bring into view how they depend on one another. The laboratory is the artificial setting in which the study of how isolated features of natural phenomena vary with one another is undertaken. Insofar as scientific method relies on abstracting such features so as to study their variations, it is guided by the assumption that these variations occur always and everywhere in the same way, which gives rise to the idea of nature being governed by laws that are universal.

Experimentation points toward mathematization, because the discovery *that* one feature varies with another leads to the question of *how exactly* it does. This question presupposes a distinction between the feature and a respect in which it can be varied while leaving the feature intact, that is between quality and quantity. Mathematization consist in assigning a quantitative range to a feature, that is treating it as a variable, and modelling the dependencies between variables by way of mathematical functions. Mathematization points back to experimentation, because the assignment of numerical values to a variable attains a physical meaning only on condition that this assignment acquires some sort of real significance. The experimental procedure which provides physical magnitudes with real significance is measurement. To provide variables with physical significance mathematized science doesn't necessarily rely on *actual* experiment and measurement. Physical insight can as well be gained by way of thought experiments inquiring into the conditions upon which measurement could be undertaken. Therefore, even theoretical physics has an experimental side to it. Moreover, even theoretical physics relies on experience. For it proceeds from the given fact that nature is characterized by certain basic magnitudes such as space, time, mass, or temperature. The empirical assumptions of mathematized science transpire most clearly from its most rigorous – axiomatic – mode of presentation: Definitions of fundamental magnitudes reveal which basic

---

[6] Cf. $20,236^{5\text{-}8}$; $9,139^{1}\text{–}166^{35}$. [7] Cf. $24.2,775^{12\text{-}15}$.

features of nature are empirically taken for granted, while axioms state quantitative correlations between these that are taken to be obvious.

Around 1800, both theoretical and empirical physics as well as emerging disciplines such as chemistry or comparative anatomy were characterized by the scientific method as outlined earlier, with varying emphasis on mathematization and experiment.[8] While biology and geology, insofar as they proceeded descriptively rather than by way of experiment and mathematization, still largely followed the traditional paradigm of natural history, what was distinctively modern about them is the striving for systematic and all-encompassing classification.[9]

Having outlined certain basic traits of the modern sciences of nature, we can now look at how these features give rise to questions which only a philosophical approach to nature can tackle. That science studies universal correlations between isolated features of nature gives rise to the question of how to justify the assumption that there are *universal* laws of nature in the first place. More concretely, the mathematical form of such laws can make one wonder how to explain the mathematizability of natural phenomena which is taken for granted by science rather than argued for. Such questions concerning the foundations of *natural science* are at the heart of Kant's philosophy of nature. Questions about mathematizability and the form of physical law can either be asked with regard to spatiotemporal phenomena in general or with regard to such phenomena insofar as they involve matter in motion. While the former are logical questions, on Kant's understanding, the latter fall into the purview of philosophy of nature proper.[10]

Kant's philosophy of nature takes mathematized physics *as it stands* and seeks to provide it with philosophical *foundations* by justifying its metaphysical presuppositions as well as the content of its definitions and axioms. By Hegel's standards modern scientific knowledge of nature is *limited* due to its method and thus needs rather to be *complemented* by a philosophical approach to *nature* that brings into view something crucial about nature that science has to pass by. Paradoxically, what natural science has to pass by due to its form of cognition is *nature as such*. It does so in two interrelated respects:

(i) Insofar as science proceeds from isolated features of the physical universe in order to gain insight into lawful correlations between them it cannot envisage what is distinctive of nature *as a whole*. It might seem, however, that science, even while not *proceeding* from the concept of nature *arrives* at a conception of what nature on the whole is, namely, the totality of lawfully correlated features which it brings into view. There are many natural sciences, though, which are in

---

[8] Cf. Stichweh 1984.   [9] Cf. Lepenies 1978.   [10] See AA9,139–166.

fact, and, according to Hegel, also in principle, irreducible to one another. If there are necessarily multiple sciences of nature, the concept of nature, that is of the natural *universe* that is studied by all those sciences, cannot be provided by any of them. Accordingly, the concept of nature isn't a scientific, but a philosophical concept.[11]

(ii) Experiment and mathematization proceed by isolating features of the physical universe in order to study lawful correlations between them. Doing so allows to bring real connections into view, to discover, for instance, how the solubility of a chemical substance depends on temperature, or how the velocity of a falling body changes with time. However, the *artificial* act of isolation that is essential to science precludes it from understanding how what has been isolated is embedded into nature as a whole, that is from comprehending its "place in nature." With regard to experimentation this means, for instance, that the *isolation* of chemical substances and the *artificial* initiation of chemical reactions between them *in the laboratory* leaves open the question which chemical reactions actually occur in nature as well as where they can occur. While questions of the aforementioned sort can still be scientifically addressed by way of cooperation between the sciences, for example between chemistry and astrophysics, there is something about the unity of the physical universe that constitutively eludes science. Mathematized physics proceeds from *multiple* basic magnitudes such as space, time, and mass in order to study quantitative dependencies between them.[12] It thereby takes for granted that all of these basic features pertain to the physical universe. However, this leaves open whether it is a contingent fact that the physical universe exhibits all of them. Science is thus constitutively precluded from giving a *principled and unconditional* answer to questions such as whether there could be a world that is spatial but not temporal, or spatial and temporal but immaterial.[13] Crucially, scientific theories *logically conjoin* multiple fundamental traits of nature, for example by proceeding from one definition *and* another, or from one axiom *and* another. One therefore needs to ask for the *real correlate* of the *logical conjunction* of fundamental traits of nature from which science proceeds. Insofar as the natural universe does not *consist* of thoughts, its basic features cannot be related to one another in the way thoughts can be related, for example by logical connectives, but must exhibit *real* connections. It is therefore a central task for the philosophy of nature as Hegel understands it to envisage nature as a *real* unity of traits that are

---

[11] On the concept of nature and its historical development, cf. Spaemann 1972; Mittelstrass 1981; Hadot 2004.
[12] Cf. on this topic Hertz 1899, 1–45.
[13] On the possibility of an empty universe from the vantage point of modern science cf. Barrow 2001.

essentially interrelated, while the natural sciences proceed from a plurality of such traits without being able to show that nature involves all of them *essentially.*[14]

According to Hegel, premodern philosophy of nature as epitomized in Aristotle's writings on the natural world incorporated an understanding of the real unity of nature, indeed. Hegel therefore qualifies the claim that philosophy of nature is a "young discipline," stressing that in a certain sense it is, while in another it isn't. This does not mean, however, that Hegel's philosophy of nature is a *patchwork* of ancient and distinctively modern strands of thinking about nature.[15]

Aristotelian science of nature prioritized being over thought insofar as it does not proceed by *artificially* isolating *features* of natural phenomena so as to bring into view their *lawful* correlations. It rather seeks to *describe* and *account for* the behavior of finite substances, that is relatively self-standing particulars which present themselves in ordinary experience. Aristotle views philosophy of nature as second rather than first philosophy, since an account of *natural* substances, that is bodies that move and change on their own initiative, presupposes a metaphysical account of *substance in general.*[16] Aristotle's account of substance is hylomorphic in that he distinguishes between form as that which accounts for the unity of a substance, and matter in the sense of that which is united and explained by form. Substantial form, in turn, is conceived of as the characteristic activity that provides for a substance's unity such as the activity of life does with regard to biological substances.[17]

According to Hegel, Aristotelian science of nature is an intimate blend of empirical and philosophical investigations. It is empirical in virtue of its descriptive uptake of features of the natural world, and nonempirical insofar

---

[14] The modern scientific approach to nature raises further questions which have been addressed in Kantian and post-Kantian philosophy. By focusing on features of nature whose variations on one another can be articulated in the form of law, natural science seems to bypass traits of nature which defy such articulation. Both Kant and Hegel assume that among such traits there are some which lie beyond the purview of science, because they owe their existence to an interplay between natural phenomena and powers of the mind beyond the power of theoretical cognition, for example natural beauty. While Kant and, to a lesser extent, Hegel, take seriously the fact that nature can be aesthetically appealing, neither of them deems this fact to be a topic for philosophy of nature, narrowly conceived.

[15] Detailed references to critical reactions of Hegel's contemporaries and subsequent readers to his attempt at synthesizing modern and premodern accounts of nature can be found in Petry 1970, 114–121.

[16] Aristotelian metaphysics or first philosophy prioritizes being over thought insofar as it investigates what belongs to being purely as such. Even while Aristotle claims that the science of being qua being and the science of the principles of thinking, logic, are one, the reason he gives, exhibits the priority of being over thought: logic is said to be part of metaphysics, because logical laws universally pertain to what is (see *Metaphysics* 1005a21–24).

[17] Cf. Kosman 2013, 69–182.

as it investigates these features by way of thinking. A material substance, in Aristotle's sense, involves a "nature" or "an inner principle of movement and rest",[18] that is one it has not been artificially endowed with. The concept of a material substance points beyond itself to the concept of an "environment" (*periechon*) which allows it to engage in its characteristic activity. Material substances are finite insofar as the characteristic processes prescribed by their own nature can only occur if appropriate conditions obtain in their environment. Man for instances, reproduces thanks to its own nature "and the sun," according to Aristotle.[19] Even while starting locally with an account of the behavior of finite substances in specific regions of the cosmos, Aristotle's philosophy of nature seeks to bring the real unity of the natural universe into view.[20] This is possible insofar as natural substances of one kind point beyond themselves to substances of other kinds whose activity allows the former to engage in their own business. The Aristotelian cosmos is thus a teleological unity, though one that is neither uniform nor exhibited as a necessary one: It is segmented into two categorically different regions, the terrestrial and the celestial region, and celestial substances are taken to be independent of the terrestrial ones for whose characteristic activities they provide conditions.

Post-Kantian philosophy of nature differs profoundly from the Aristotelian view of nature in at least two respects which align it with modern science. It prioritizes thought over being insofar as it proceeds from the question of how it might even be possible to know something about nature by way of thinking *alone*, rather than by observation and experience. Modern philosophy of nature is accordingly based on a philosophical conception of thought and its relation to being, that is on a logic with metaphysical import. While Kant and Hegel agree with Aristotle that philosophy of nature is second rather than first philosophy, they conceive of first philosophy as the self-knowledge of pure thought in relation to being, rather than first and foremost as an account of being as such. Moreover, post-Kantian philosophy of nature proceeds from abstract, global features of the natural universe such as space, time, matter, and motion, rather than from natural substances, that is bodies in motion.

These distinctively modern features notwithstanding, what aligns Hegel's philosophy of nature with Aristotle's is the quest for the unity of nature.[21] Hegel conceives of modern science as *constitutively* incomplete insofar as it proceeds from a *multiplicity* of isolated features of nature with the intent to study their lawful variation with one another. This, however, presupposes that what varies

---

[18] Aristotle, *Physics* 192b13–14. [19] Aristotle, *Physics* 194b13. Cf. Wieland 1992, 231–253.
[20] Cf. Falcon 2005.
[21] Cf. Ferrarin 1998. For Hegel's inheritance of Platonist and Renaissance philosophy see Magee 2001.

with one another in ways which wait to be discovered already belongs to one and the same universe. A *universe* cannot be an aggregate, that is a multiplicity of independent items which happen to be connected by way of external relations. In order to be thus connectable, these items would have to already partake in a prior unity that cannot itself be an aggregate.

To exhibit nature as a *universe* it accordingly doesn't suffice to state, for instance, that nature is spatial, *and* temporal, *and* material,[22] while also stating how such features have been *found* to vary with one another. One rather needs to bring into view the *primordial unity* between such features that underlies their quantifiable correlations. This unity cannot be an additive one, that is it cannot consist in external relations between space, time, matter etc. Hegel's philosophy of nature thus aligns itself with the ancient Aristotelian conception of nature, seeking to exhibit nature as a "living whole"[23] – not in the sense of taking it to be literally alive, but in the sense of its being a totality, that is a whole that comprises essentially interrelated traits rather than being composed of parts that could have an independent standing on their own.

1.2 The Logical, Nature, and Spirit

According to Hegel neither the concept nor the existence of nature can be taken for granted, philosophically. Insofar as it designates a *totality* that does *not* consist of thoughts the concept of nature is neither an empirical nor a logical concept. The only way to acquire *philosophical*, that is *nonempirical* knowledge of such a totality must be an *indirect* one, following upon an inquiry into thought purely as such, that is logic. *Logic,* on Hegel's understanding is the systematic study of those thoughts which have their source in the intellect alone and which do not, as such, *specifically* address that which does not consist of thoughts, that is the realm of things. On Hegel's conception, *logic* has ontological import insofar as it unfolds the *notion* of being, exhibiting in pure thought the determinations that belong to being purely as such.[24] Even while logical concepts such as *quality* and *quantity* therefore have a *bearing* on what there is such concepts do not purport to be about things *rather than thoughts*: Quality and quantity, for instance, pertain to both thoughts and things, while not specifically addressing either.

Hegel calls the totality of logical determinations "the logical" while referring to the concept of this totality as the "logical idea." Not all pure thoughts are logical ones. For the concept of a realm that does not consist of thoughts, that is

---

[22] Cf. Hegel's claim that philosophy "fights the And" (*bekämpft das Auch*, TW9, 487 A.); see also 24.1,194[5-22].
[23] 20,241[14]; 24.1,191[13]; 24.2,946[10-13]; 24.2,976[13].
[24] Cf. Houlgate 2006; Martin 2012; Koch, 2014; Pippin 2018.

the concept of reality, is a pure concept, albeit a non-logical one. The step that leads from the logical idea to the concept of reality is thus a step from one kind of philosophical discipline to another, namely, from "logic" to "the real sciences of philosophy",[25] as Hegel puts it.

It might be objected, however, that Hegel is notorious for taking "reason" to be "in the world".[26] This might seem to mean that there isn't anything which is not a thought, on his account. The conceptual is "unbounded," the world is thoughts "all the way down," or so the story goes.[27] This cannot be quite right, though, for if Hegel didn't reckon with anything beyond pure thoughts logic would have to be the only philosophical discipline. That Hegel distinguishes between "logic" and the "real sciences of philosophy" indicates that he doesn't simply equate thoughts and things.

The reason why Hegel speaks of "real sciences of philosophy" in the plural is that one can distinguish between the real *purely as such*, that is nature, and the real *insofar as* it is shaped and acted upon by embodied thinking, that is the world of spirit. Nature is accordingly the realm of things rather than thoughts *insofar as* this realm has not been shaped by embodied thinking.

A precondition of grasping the relations between the logical, nature, and spirit consists in clearly distinguishing between these, on the one hand, and the philosophical disciplines dealing with them, on the other. Logic, philosophy of nature, and philosophy of spirit are all cognitive activities on the part of embodied thinkers and thus fall into the realm of spirit, while the topics of logic and philosophy of nature have something about them which doesn't. When asking about the relation between the logical and nature one thus needs to take precaution to not conflate this relation with the relation between logic and philosophy of nature. Notably, the fact that there is a "transition" in philosophical thinking from logic to philosophy of nature does not imply that the relation between the logical and nature has the character of a "transition" whatever that might mean.[28]

In places Hegel suggests that the logical idea grounds nature by timelessly turning itself into it. His formulations are heavily metaphorical for which reason both their sense and their rationale remain disputed. He speaks of the idea as "externalizing itself" (*sich entäußern*[29]) as nature or "resolving itself" (*sich entschließen*[30]) to be nature. One might worry that such formulations are at odds with his insight that nature is a realm that does not consist of thoughts and thus cannot have its sufficient ground in thought. That nature is a realm that does not consist of or contain thoughts is acknowledged in Hegel's characterization of it

---

[25] 21,9$^{2-4}$, cf. 24.1,771$^{21-22}$. [26] 21.35^7. [27] See McDowell 1996, 24–45.
[28] Cf. Martin 2021, 93–97. See also Olvera and Reyes 2021. [29] 21,57$^{21-22}$.
[30] 20,231$^{21-22}$.

as "the other of the idea" (*das Andere der Idee*[31]). This characterization does not imply that nature is alien to thought. Even while not *consisting* of thoughts the realm of nature is essentially *intelligible*. It is, because something unintelligible would still be *something*, and Hegel's logic shows that something as such lends itself to be cognized in accord with a whole system of logical concepts which go hand in hand with the category of *something*.[32] That nature does not *consist* of thoughts, while not being alien to thought either, is manifest in Hegel's inchoate conception of it as the logical "idea in the form of otherness."[33] That nature is said to be the idea in *another form* indicates that nature is intelligible, while exhibiting *another kind of unity* than thoughts have. Hegel characterizes this way by referring to nature as the "immediate idea"[34] or, more vividly, following Schelling, as "petrified intelligence."[35] Roughly speaking, these formulations indicate that nature involves thoughts indeed, but in a "densely packed" way, so to speak, which is categorically different from their occurrence as discrete contents of acts of thinking. Putting things this way is somewhat misleading, though, insofar as it still suggests that nature somehow "consists" of thoughts, albeit indiscriminately. Its distinctively non-logical mode of being is more aptly expressed by Hegel's claim that nature exhibits the "form of otherness"[36] or "externality".[37] While pure thoughts are characterized by "internality" insofar as each of them is both distinct from the others and systematically interrelated with them, "otherness" or "externality" means that nature is a realm that *allows* for things that are independent of and thus external to each other.

That otherness or externality is a fundamental trait of nature does not mean, however, that nature *is* an array of items that are externally related to each other. Only things which already belong to one and the same universe can be externally related. In the first instance, nature's externality must therefore be *absolute* rather than *relative*: Nature is the realm of that which is external *to itself*. What is external *to itself* is such that it is *on its own* already *beyond itself*. Insofar as nature is the realm of *self*-externality, it is a continuum.[38] For a continuum is a manifold that does not consist of a determinate number of items but is such that any *section* of it points beyond itself and is, accordingly, *on its own* seamlessly embedded into that which it is *not*, that is its surroundings.

That nature is, most fundamentally, a continuous manifold renders concrete the claim that it does not consist of thoughts, even while being intelligible. For *thought* is a count noun and the logical is thus a system of internally related units that can be counted, while a continuum is a manifold that does not consist of a determinate number of well-distinguished elements and thus cannot be

---

[31] $24.1,209^{13}$; $24.1,507^{13}$;510^{12-14}.   [32] Cf. $21,102^{20}-104^{18}$.   [33] $20,237^3$.
[34] $20,231^{13}$; $24.1,8^{11-12}$.   [35] TW9,25A.   [36] $20,237^3$; $24.1,516^{1-2}$.   [37] $20,60^{12}$.
[38] Cf. $20,243^{15-19}$; $24.1,14^{14-19}$; $24.1,228^{10-16}$.

counted. However, there is nothing unintelligible about a continuum insofar as it *allows* to single out discrete elements or subsections by way of thinking. That there isn't anything about the real as such that cannot be cognized doesn't imply, though, that nature could ever be exhausted by thought, for a continuum is such as to always allow to draw further distinctions. Such distinctions might very well be subordinate and repetitive, however. This is why nature, even while logically inexhaustible, might still be exhaustively cognizable with regard to its global, essential traits.

That the real is the "other" of the logical that cannot in principle be exhausted by thought entails that nature is marked by contingency, that is real independence. Insofar as it is marked by contingency, the continuum must be inhomogeneous, that is its continuous way of hanging together must vary *irregularly* in places. The relation between determinate traits of nature cannot exclusively be marked by contingency, though, because otherwise it would lack a real unity. If nature's continuous way of hanging together varies irregularly in places, this gives rise to neighboring sections of the continuum whose determinate traits are independent of one another. However, such neighboring sections must still be tied to each other by some sort of *real* connection rather than one that is merely thought. Their real connection cannot consist in an immediate juxtaposition of determinations that are independent of one another, because this would in fact amount to a lack of real connection. The real connection in question must rather involve a coincidence of opposites which is as such instable and *must* therefore result in something that resolves the tension. Accordingly, even while things in nature aren't related to each other internally, there must nonetheless be some sort of local necessary connection between them that goes hand in hand with their contingent distribution across the continuum. Nature is thus marked by contingency *and* necessity.[39] The latter is a formal feature of something that brings about the subsequent existence of something else without itself containing determinate recourse to what it brings about. What is connected as cause and effect is still external to each other, since the tension that brings about the effect that resolves it does not itself *determinately foreshadow* its effect before bringing it about.

Nature accordingly involves a dimension that allows for contingent relations and a dimension along which items follow upon each other necessarily, that is space and time. That nature is marked by contingency *and* necessity entails that fundamental features of nature will be both *relatively* independent and *globally* dependent on one another. Matter and motion, for instance, are relatively independent of one another: Insofar as matter is inert, it is indifferent to being

---

[39] See 20,237[9-12].

in motion or at rest. Whether a chunk of matter is in motion or at rest will thus depend on something beyond that very chunk. However, even while matter can indeed be in a state of motion or rest that is accidental to it, motion and matter cannot be *generally* independent of one another, because otherwise they would lack real unity. The external transmission of motion by way of impact, for instance, will thus be subordinate to and dependent on motion that is not accidental to matter, but has its real ground in matter itself, namely, gravitational motion. The relative local independence of matter and motion that presupposes their global dependence can be illustrated by a billiard ball that *externally* impacts on another while the earth on which it does is moving lawfully *on its own initiative* around the sun.

The necessary connections between things in nature do not involve internal relations between these, given that nature is a realm of externality. What is spatially and temporally extended is real. Insofar as nature involves *necessary* connections between spatiotemporally extended things, these connections themselves aren't real in the sense of being spatiotemporally extended, but ideal. The ideal in nature is that which is involved in the necessary connections between things, while not itself being spatially and temporally extended, even while being real in the broad sense of not being a mere thought. The point which is the center of mass of a body toward which another body falls is something ideal *in nature*, rather than being something merely subjective or imaginary. As Hegel stresses, both real and ideal features of nature pertain to nature itself. Such features can even "stand in" for each other in that the variation of a real feature can have the same consequences as the variation of an ideal feature. The force a moving body can exert will, for instance, be raised by increasing its mass as well as by increasing its velocity.[40]

The *way* in which determinate features of things depend on and vary with one another is not itself a real feature of things, but an ideal one. Such a way is universal insofar as equal causes bring about equal effects. A universal correlation between features of things in nature is a law of nature. A law of nature captures an ideal aspect *of nature itself*, rather than *just* being situated on the level of thinking about nature. The law cannot, however, be found in space and time, since it is a *general way* in which spatially extended things change. Cognizing a law of nature thus involves a translation, so to speak, from the way in which sections of the continuum change to the discrete thought of such a way. On the level of nature there is nothing over and above the way in which particular subsections of the continuum change, while a law of nature is independent of any recourse to particulars.[41] The law thus neither mirrors

---

[40] See 20,253$^{3\text{-}14}$.   [41] Cf. 24.1,5$^{14\text{-}15}$.

something that is there anyway nor does it merely project something onto nature that is alien to it. It rather renders in a discrete form a distinctive kind of unity between things in nature which does not have discrete existence on the part of nature itself. Cognition of nature thus involves the discrete articulation of features of the inhomogeneous continuum of nature by way of general concepts. It thereby invests nature with internal relations insofar as its concepts are internally related to each other by way of the laws in which they figure. Laws of nature are thus neither simply "in" nature nor merely subjective, but have their proper place in *knowledge* of nature. A law of nature can thus be objectively valid without just mirroring something that obtains anyway.

Laws of nature, insofar as they pertain to global traits of nature such as space, time, motion, and mass, cannot be wholly contingent. The natural universe would otherwise lack real unity. Insofar as laws of nature aren't contingent, it must be possible to know them a priori. Such laws must have a quantitative side, because they regulate the variation of relations between features of a space-time-continuum, and quantity is what allows for continuous variation. It must thus be possible to know a priori, and hence philosophically, that certain basic traits of nature vary with one another. On the other hand, there must be something contingent about laws of nature, because nature is marked by both necessity and contingency. What cannot be known a priori and thus cannot be known philosophically are the *determinate* quantitative relations between the magnitudes involved in a law of nature. Quantities can be increased or decreased by *externally* adding more of the same. Determinate quantities therefore cannot be arrived at by self-determining thought thinking nature. There must rather be something matter-of-factual about them. One might therefore be wary that Hegel's attempt to philosophically deduce certain mathematical laws of classical mechanics such as Kepler's laws[42] – an attempt which he himself viewed as collateral to the core task of philosophy of nature – goes beyond the proper bounds of philosophy of nature.

As we have seen, nature is a realm of externality that involves law-governed interactions between things. Even while the things themselves are only externally rather than internally related, they can be more or less organized and their interrelations can be more or less involved. The philosophy of nature thus unfolds a series of ever more complex concepts pertaining to levels of ever more intimate organization on the part of nature. Nature is thus exhibited as a "series of stages".[43] This series reveals an "idealization" on the part of nature itself insofar as its traits are bound up more intimately with one another on each stage.[44] Matter, for instance, insofar as it is just heavy, lacks inner articulation

---

[42] See E §230. [43] $20,238^{29}$–239^1. [44] Cf. $24.1,13^{15-16}$.

and attracts other matter indiscriminately, whereas chemical substances are internally structured and thus react with certain kinds of substance, only, while the living organism is articulated in such a way that parts of a certain *kind* can only exist within a functioning whole of a certain kind.

According to Hegel, thinking through the concept of one stage of nature leads to the concept of another. Philosophical transitions between the concepts of these stages do neither entail that one stage originates from another in time nor do they entail that one stage "grounds" the other in a timeless manner. What *really* corresponds to the *philosophical* transition between the concepts of such stages on the part of nature can only be asked with regard to one transition at a time, rather than being anticipated in a general manner.

As a realm of self-externality nature does not involve items which literally determine *themselves* in the sense of being the source of their own determinations. Only thinking can be the source of its own determinations and only thinking beings can therefore be free. The self-determination proper to thinking is neither arbitrary nor externally necessitated but consists in an *autonomous growth of determinacy*, one which can be both creative and rational.[45] Processes in nature, by contrast, are neither self-determining nor free. Nonetheless, there are things in nature whose characteristic processes are *determined from within* rather than from without, for example the motions of heavenly bodies in a solar system. The "freedom of solar systems,"[46] however, is nothing but a reflex of actual freedom in a realm in which there is no freedom, in nature.

The idealization pertaining to the successive stages of nature culminates in animal subjectivity. The animal is related to itself by being bodily presented with itself in perception and feeling. It remains immersed into externality, however, insofar as it does not distinguish between itself and its bodily states and thus lacks reflective self-determination which is essential to spirit. Hegel's account of life *and* spirit is distinctively ecological in that he doesn't conceive of them as if they could occur just anywhere in the natural universe. Life and spirit are rather tied to a certain kind of place in nature, namely, terrestrial planets.[47] Spirit is neither part of nature nor independent of nature, on Hegel's account. It is embodied self-determination that distinguishes between itself, its own kind, and its natural environment. Spirit shapes its natural environment, the Earth, in a way that transforms it into a world of shared significance.

---

[45] Cf. Martin 2012. [46] Cf. Koschel 2023.
[47] Cf. Martin 2025a for a reconstruction of Hegel's conception of terrestrial planets as the place of life in nature; Martin 2025d on the idea that the circulation of matter on a terrestrial planet is a necessary condition of life; and Martin 2024 for Hegel's view of the Earth as the natural habitat of spirit. See also fn. 204. For ecological perspectives on Hegel's philosophy of nature cf. Ferrer and Krijnen 2025.

Hegel's distinction between nature and spirit follows the Aristotelian distinction between *phýsis* and *téchne* to the extent that both have a reflective character: They do not purport to refer to independent entities but allow characterizing one and the same reality in different respects. However, the Aristotelian and the Hegelian distinction stand squarely to one another. Something is natural in Aristotle's sense insofar as it has not been made, that is insofar as it does not involve an externally implanted form.[48] Something is natural in Hegel's sense insofar as it *is determined*, be it from without or from within, rather than *determining itself* or being a result of *self-determining* activity. By Aristotle's standards, finite rational beings are natural beings, because the principle of their life, reason, is an inner principle of motion and rest that has not been externally implanted into a body. In contrast, spirit or embodied self-determination, by Hegel's standards, transcends nature, because nature is a realm of determinacy and external relations rather than of self-determination proper.

1.3 Nature and the Concept of Nature

We have just given an inchoate characterization of nature as the realm of self-externality. We have thus provided a first grip on the concept of nature. The task of philosophy of nature consists in explicating this concept, according to Hegel.[49] It is essential to not conflate nature and the concept of nature.[50] *Distinguishing* between nature and its concept does not entail *dualism*, that is a gap between them. On the contrary, drawing this distinction is a precondition of understanding how philosophy of nature can provide us with knowledge of *nature*. Philosophy of nature seeks to systematically unpack the concept of nature purely by way of thinking. The concept of nature has its place in thought about nature. It is neither spatially nor temporally extended, while nature is, nor does it bear other properties characteristic of things in nature. Nonetheless, the concept of nature captures what is essential to nature. It can only do so, because nature is a spatially and temporally extended realm that bears an essential unity, one that is not merely thought, but real. The concept of nature articulates the essential unity pertaining to nature, while not *giving* the spatiotemporal manifold that is held together by that unity. The concept of nature is thus neither alien to nature nor contained in it nor does it coincide with it. It rather reveals its form.[51]

---

[48] Aristotle, *Physics* 132b8-32. [49] Cf. 24.2,774^{12}; 24.2,776$^{3-4}$; 24.2, 958$^{21-22}$.
[50] A conflation of that sort seems to be going on in Stephen Houlgate's claim that the logical idea "grounds nature in a highly unusual manner: not by preceding it in time, but by proving itself to be nothing less than nature itself" (2006, 107). He goes on to claim that philosophy of nature has to focus on "what follows logically from nature … namely, from the very externality of space itself" (110).
[51] Cf. 24.1,509^{33}.

The concept of nature *exhibits* nature as a real unity, rather than mirroring or representing it, because the unity of nature isn't a *part* of nature, but the way in which the spatiotemporal continuum hangs together. While the unity of nature is neither separate nor separable from what it unifies, the concept of that unity is. Spatial unity, for instance, is neither separate nor separable from the spatial manifold, while the concept of spatial unity, that is the concept of space, is indeed distinguishable from space. The concept of space is therefore, so to speak, a transformed guise of the unity of the spatial, rather than simply coinciding with the latter. Pure thought of nature thus inevitably involves an intellectual "transformation" or "appropriation" of the real unity on the part of nature[52]. Philosophy of nature proceeds by immanently unfolding the inchoate concept of nature qua realm of self-externality, providing an ever more concrete conception of nature, that is of the essential unity in virtue of which the spatiotemporal universe is a *universe* indeed.

The concept of nature is the concept of a singularetantum, the natural universe. In the course of philosophically unfolding that concept, concepts of kinds of things, namely natural kind concepts will come into play. This follows from nature being an inhomogeneous continuum. An inhomogeneous continuum is one whose continuous way of hanging together varies discontinuously in places, such as at the border between a vessel and a fluid contained in it. Accordingly, certain regions of the spatiotemporal continuum will be set apart from others insofar as their internal coherence varies specifically from that of their surroundings. Concepts of natural kinds will thus pertain to *sections* of the spatial continuum which exhibit a distinctive internal unity that sets them off from their surroundings – a unity which they tend to preserve or modify in determinate ways when interacting with other such sections.

Hegel's conception of natural kinds can neither be equated with the Aristotelian understanding of substantial forms nor with Kant's conception of natures. Aristotle conceives of matter as indeterminate stuff that doesn't exist independently of bearing a certain form, where form is unificatory activity that sets a natural substance apart from its environment. Kant realized that matter cannot be distinguished from activity or force in this way, because space-filling itself must be thought as an activity and matter must thus be conceived in terms of act rather than potency. Hegel follows Kant's dynamical account of matter in

---

[52] Cf. Hegel's claims that "the form of nature" is "immediacy" ($24.1,10^{8-11}$) and "singularity" (TW9,24A.), while cognition of nature yields general distinctions (cf. $24.1,200^{29}$–201^2; $24.1,213^{4-6}$).

this regard while reproaching him with missing the unity of the activity that matter consists in due to his proceeding from a dualism of forces.

If matter *itself* is an activity rather than a potential, the natures of material particulars cannot be understood as "substantial forms" or "immanent universals," that is as consisting in some sort of unificatory activity *over and above matter* that sets a natural substance apart from its environment. What sets one material particular apart from another is a question Kant did not answer in a satisfying way. The ultimate reason for this failure, by Hegel's standards, is Kant's conception of space and time *as forms of sensibility* in distinction to matter which is viewed as "the real" in space and time.[53] This leaves Kant with a subjectivist account of the forms of things since these appear to owe their unity to synthetic activity on the part of the subject, *only*. While Kant's conception of transcendental affinity acknowledges that the real that affects the subject must at least be synthesizable,[54] he doesn't address the actual unity on the part of the real that allows a *given* manifold to be synthesized by a subject. Hegel, instead, conceives of the real as an *inhomogeneous* continuum, that is as comprising subsections that are internally held together and set apart from their surroundings thanks to the peculiar activity of matter in the respective subsection. In consequence, he doesn't conceive of natures as "substantial forms" or "immanent universals" which are supposed to be somehow "contained in" the spatiotemporal universe.[55] He views *a* nature as the specific activity *of matter* thanks to which a distinctive subsection of the spatial continuum sets itself apart from its surroundings, bearing a distinctive configuration of its own and preserving itself in the course of interaction with other things.

In consequence, Hegel does not subscribe to some sort of "conceptual realism" according to which nature somehow "contains concepts" or "immanent universals" (*logoi enhyloi*) as Aristotle has it. Neither does he subscribe to the "idealist" view that any attempt to "cut nature at the joints" must be futile insofar as it inevitably involves a *mere projection* of distinctions on our part. Instead of addressing the question of natural kinds while taking the concept of nature or objective reality for granted, Hegel first and foremost investigates the kind of unity characteristic of nature qua spatiotemporal universe, the form of reality as such. Only against that background does he envisage what being a natural kind or a particular instantiating such a kind amounts to. What it amounts to is that subsections of a continuum, while continuously embedded into their surroundings, can at the same time set themselves apart from these in

---

[53] CPR A175-6/B217.　[54] CPR A122.
[55] According to Hegel, the concept is "lost, vanished" ($24.1,281^{18\text{-}20}$), the "way" reason is in nature is "conceptless" ($24.1,510^{12\text{-}14}$). If at all, the concept exists in nature "in a different manner" ($24.2,951^{34}$–952^{1}) or a different "form" ($24.2,953^{31}$), namely, the form laid out earlier.

virtue of how their inner coherence differs from that of their surroundings. The graph of a continuous albeit non-differentiable function provides a geometrical model for this: It comprises well-distinguishable, albeit continuous, subsections due to its continuity varying in a discontinuous manner in the places in which it is bent.

If one doesn't take the underlying continuous nature of the physical universe seriously, imagining it to be a discrete manifold or a set as is customary in contemporary analytic metaphysics, then it might indeed seem that nature or reality must somehow contain "immanent concepts" or "universals".[56] This view is problematic, though. In any event, nature, as a realm of particulars, cannot consist of concepts or universals *only*. Saying that nature "contains" concepts or "immanent universals" raises the question of how the unity between these concepts and what they are supposed to be "immanent" in should be understood. What they are immanent in cannot itself involve concepts, because that would amount to a regress. The habitat of "immanent universals" would therefore have to be *altogether* non-conceptual and, thus, unintelligible. The view of nature or reality as containing "immanent universals" therefore entails a sort of dualism: It makes the physical universe fall apart into "immanent" concepts and something wholly unintelligible.

The question of how "immanent concepts" are "in" nature is bypassed rather than addressed by the claim that reality is "conceptually structured".[57] A structure is a set of items and relations between them. Sets and structures aren't real, even while their elements might indeed be *sections* of reality. The sets and structures themselves are abstract objects which owe their existence to thought. That a particular instantiates a *natural* kind means that it does not owe its unity to *thought*. Appearances to the contrary, rather than giving us a grip on the unity of things in nature, the view of "immanent universals" and of nature as "conceptually structured" thus in fact subjectivizes things.

On Hegel's account, cognition of nature and of natures does not, accordingly, consist in adequately "representing" or "mirroring" "structures" or "immanent universals" "contained" in nature. Hegel takes recourse to a number of telling metaphors which make clear that cognizing natural kinds and objects instantiating them involves an *articulation* or *transformation* of the way in which regions of the spatiotemporal continuum set themselves apart from their surroundings. Cognizing nature requires a "metamorphosis,"[58] "assimilation,"[59] "appropriation"[60] or "liberation"[61] of the characteristic unity of a subsection of the continuous manifold by means of discursive concepts which have their only

---

[56] Kreines 2015, 22.   [57] Stern 2018, 110; cf. Kreines 2015, 23.   [58] $24.1,198^{7-9}$.
[59] $24.2,937^{27}$.   [60] $24.1,5^{19-22}$; $24.1,202^{15-16}$.   [61] $24.1,201^2$.

place in the logical act of cognition itself. That a discursive concept has its only place in the act of cognition does not in any way subjectivize concepts, because the paradigmatic contribution of a concept to the act of cognition consists in articulating how things are. As Hegel insists, knowledge of nature does neither mirror "structures" on the part of nature itself nor does it merely project distinctions onto nature. It is neither identical nor different from what is known, but is related to it by "identity-in-difference" insofar as it is an articulation of what is in itself essentially articulable.[62]

Neither philosophy nor science seeks to know particulars for their own sake, but each provides us with general insight into nature. According to Hegel, both science and philosophy of nature have "the same universal as their topic" (*dasselbe Allgemeine*), while their "ways of knowing" differ.[63] In which way they do and how science and philosophy of nature may be seen as complementing each other shall now be addressed.

1.4 Philosophy of Nature and the Natural Sciences

While the natural universe is a particular, the topic of both science and philosophy of nature is something general rather than particular: It is the kind of unity that pertains to nature, the kinds of things belonging to it and the kinds of relations obtaining between them. Knowledge of reality involves logical concepts, on Hegel's account. It is a result of his *Logic* that the objective world is an inhomogeneous continuum that is organized on various levels to which different kinds of logical form of articulation correspond.[64] In virtue of its inner organization the objective world cannot be comprehensively accounted for by one science, only, but requires an interplay of various sciences that are irreducible to each other insofar as they avail themselves of different logical forms of cognition, namely, those of mechanism, chemism, and teleology. The sciences that avail themselves of these logical forms, namely, physics, chemistry, biology, and geology complement each other in the following way: They do not necessarily pertain to disjoint sections of the natural universe, but rather to different levels of organization that can overlap. While the laws pertaining to a lower level of organization apply *ubiquitously* to all objects including those situated on higher levels of organization, the behavior of these more organized objects is not completely determined by that of the less organized ones.[65] While animals, for instance, are subject to the laws of fall or the laws of chemistry in the same

---

[62] Cf. $24.1,191^{3-5}$; $24.1,215^{20}-216^{1}$.   [63] $24.1,187^{3-5}$; $24.2,940^{23-24}$.

[64] Physics, chemistry, and biology are in principle irreducible, because they are all modes of objective cognition which employ different logical forms of explanation as laid out in the *SoL* (12,133–191). Cf. Martin 2012, 354–413.

[65] Cf. Hendry 2010, 188.

way as inorganic bodies are, they also exhibit behavior that isn't fully determined and therefore cannot be explained by recourse to physical or chemical laws.

As Hegel points out, philosophy of nature differs from the natural sciences not so much by its topic but by its "way of knowing." Philosophy seeks to cognize nature by way of pure thinking, unfolding the concept of nature so as to arrive at an ever more concrete understanding of nature's unity. The sciences, on the other hand, know nature in a way that involves external givenness, that is recourse to experience. What is distinctive of scientific knowledge, on Hegel's account, is that science connects concepts pertaining to the natural world without arriving at these concepts in the way philosophy does, namely, by proceeding from the inchoate concept of nature qua self-externality and thinking through what self-externality entails.

Independently of their specific methods, all natural sciences proceed from a logical conjunction of concepts and assertions. Nature or the real as such, however, does not consist of thoughts and thus cannot itself be united by way of logical connectives. There must accordingly be a real unity on the part of nature that corresponds to the logical unity in the foundations of science. Insofar as science *proceeds* from a logical conjunction of concepts and assertions, it is barred from ever envisaging the *primordial* unity on the part of nature in virtue of which there is a spatiotemporal *universe* in the first place. Science can *approach* the real unity of nature by way of theory unification, while it cannot *reach* it without ceasing to be science. Moreover, if there are inevitably multiple sciences marked by different, irreducible forms of cognition and explanation, the body of scientific knowledge of nature inevitably amounts to a logical conjunction of *theories*. What the natural sciences can indeed do, while philosophy cannot, is gaining ever more concrete insight into the *lawful but contingent* aspects of the real unity of nature. If theoretical physics, for instance, *proceeds* from the concepts of space, time, and mass, it must leave open the question whether there could be a universe which is merely spatial, or one that involves space and matter only, or one that is merely temporal. Even while physics envisages lawful quantitative connections between space, time, and motion, that there are such lawful connections must appear as a brute fact from the vantage point of science.

The endemic logicism of science not only prevents us from grasping the primordial unity of nature which only philosophy can address. A logical concatenation of basic magnitudes can even distort the scientific understanding of these magnitudes and their quantitative dependencies. The unfinished path that leads from classical to modern physics not only involves a unification of theories thanks to the reduction of the number of independent principles. It also does away with distortions in scientific approaches to nature which are due to unreflectively contenting oneself with a mere logical juxtaposition of basic magnitudes without raising the question of the real unity between these. Asking this question can make one see, for instance, that space, time, and motion cannot be conceived as absolute, but need to be conceived of as relative, indeed. There is thus a *philosophical* tendency in physics itself, for example in the path from Newton's to Einstein's account of space, time, and matter. However, even while science rids itself of certain logicist fallacies, logicism as such remains endemic to science for the reason indicated.

The endemic logicism of science isn't limited to the *theoretical* side of science. *Experimental* science, such as experimental chemistry, isolates certain features of matter and investigates their correlations in the *artificial setting* of the *laboratory*. In consequence it juxtaposes its topic with the rest of nature: It leaves open whether its subject matter has a real place in nature and where in the physical universe it belongs. Experimental chemistry, for instance, leaves open whether certain chemical reactions it artificially initiates do indeed occur in nature and, if so, where.

That philosophy of nature addresses questions which the natural sciences have to leave open, namely, questions pertaining to the primordial nonquantitative unity between fundamental magnitudes, does not mean that the sciences would be deficient as long as they have not been given a philosophical foundation. In order to mathematically and experimentally investigate nature science has to proceed in the way it does. Philosophy of nature, however, can help to clarify science by bringing out how it relies, in certain regards, on logical abstractions, which make it a limited model of nature, rather than a full blown account of its real unity. Addressing a logical connection on the level of science to which a real counterpart is as of yet lacking can allow to remedy this sort of defect scientifically, for example by unifying hitherto separated theories or by conceiving of how one magnitude (e.g. duration or length) which was taken to be independent of another (e.g. velocity) actually varies with it. Since a logical conjunction of basic concepts and assumptions is constitutive of science, asking quasi-philosophical questions about the real counterparts of logical connections cannot result in doing away with these altogether and turn science into a completely unified account of nature. It will rather reveal that any scientific account of nature will be lacking as an account of its primordial necessary unity.[66] Any philosophical account of nature, on the other hand, will be found lacking as an account of its empirical, quantitatively determinate unity.

---

[66] Cf. 24.1,490$^{27\text{-}29}$.

To the question whether philosophy of nature depends on natural science Hegel replies that the "genesis" and "formation" of philosophy of nature indeed presuppose science.[67] Some interpreters take this to mean that scientific insights are an enabling condition of philosophy of nature, only, while not being an essential part of it.[68] It should thus in principle be possible to engage in philosophy of nature independently of knowing any science. Other interpreters stress that philosophy of nature is indeed dependent on scientific cognition of nature insofar as it is a kind of second-order reflection that seeks to reconstruct "basic paradigms" at work in the practices of the sciences themselves.[69] While the first view makes they way in which philosophy of nature depends on science too external, the second view makes it so tight that philosophy of nature is done away with in favor of a peculiar brand of philosophy of science, namely, one that is supposed to be guided by Hegel's *Logic*. On the first view it becomes impossible to understand that philosophy of nature, as any part of philosophy, has a history that is philosophically revealing, and one at that which is entangled with the history of science. It then becomes hard to grasp why fundamental concepts of modern theoretical physics, for example the concepts of energy, of time dilation, or of quanta, do not appear in Hegel's philosophy of nature. Claiming that these concepts, from the vantage point of philosophy of nature, all pertain to contingent aspects of nature rather than touching upon its primordial unity as envisaged in Hegel's philosophy of nature would be missing the point. For thermodynamics, relativity theory and quantum physics do not merely investigate subordinate phenomena but concern the global outlook of nature.

It would be premature, though, to conclude from this that philosophy of nature can only be some sort of second-order reflection on forms of thought and explanation that are at work in the sciences. For it then becomes unintelligible that philosophy of nature can indeed delve deeper, in certain respects, than the sciences at a certain time could. One thus bereaves oneself of understanding how Hegel could *rationally* anticipate certain insights of special relativity[70] or how Schelling could have come up with the idea of electromagnetism before its empirical discovery.[71]

To become clear about how philosophy of nature relies on empirical science without inheriting its empirical character, we have to take seriously Hegel's claim that philosophy "takes up" concepts pertaining to nature in the shape in which science provides them and then "transforms" this "material" "without

---

[67] 20,236[13-19]. [68] Cf. Maker 1998, 17; Stone 2005, 1–28; Houlgate 2006, 116.
[69] Cf. Pinkard 2004, 26; see also Rand 2007, 395; Rand 2017, 391–392.
[70] Cf. Wandschneider 1982; Wandschneider 1986; Wandschneider 1987.
[71] Cf. Friedman 2007.

relying on experience".[72] With regard to scientific concepts of basic traits of nature it can be asked whether these traits pertain to nature just contingently or necessarily and, if so, what their necessary connection consists in. By providing philosophy with concepts pertaining to basic traits of nature science bequeaths it with a kind of question that only philosophy can answer, namely, whether there is a necessary primordial unity between these traits. An affirmative answer to a question of that sort can only be a nonempirical one, and it thus does away with the impression that the concepts in question pertain to contingent traits of nature which can only be known empirically.

Philosophy of nature doesn't ask such questions in a haphazard way. It rather seeks to arrive at an integrated conception of fundamental traits of nature by proceeding in an orderly fashion. In the process of discovery it can take its point of departure from concepts of such traits as they occur in science. However, it seeks to purify these concepts by deriving philosophical counterparts of theirs which Hegel calls "conceptual determinations" (*Begriffsbestimmungen*). The philosophical concepts it arrives at will thus not simply coincide with their scientific counterparts. The philosophical concept can shed light on the corresponding scientific concept insofar as it clarifies its nonempirical marks and the way these hang together both among each other and with further concepts. The philosophical way with a natural-scientific concept yields a pure content that is articulated in nonscientific terms. A conceptual determination of that sort, for example the idea of "immediate self-externality," thus needs to be matched with "the empirical appearance which corresponds to it,"[73] that is space, in the case at hand.[74] By "empirical appearance" Hegel does not mean some kind of brute intuition, but a phenomenon insofar as it is articulated in scientific language, for example the content of the word "space" as it occurs in science which elaborates on ordinary prescientific usage of that word.

1.5 The Task and the Method of Hegel's Philosophy of Nature

The task of Hegel's philosophy of nature is to systematically develop the inchoate conception of nature as self-externality so as to achieve a concrete understanding of the essential unity that obtains between fundamental traits of nature. It promises to thereby overcome the moment of mere juxtaposition characteristic of scientific concepts of nature, their theoretical interconnection notwithstanding.[75] By thinking through the inchoate conception of nature as self-externality it reveals that the natural universe must exhibit the determinate traits designated by those concepts. It is thus by way of the

---

[72] TW9,20 A.; 24.1,490$^{17-26}$.   [73] 20,236$^{19-20}$, cf. 20,278$^{8-14}$.   [74] 24.1,243$^{15-17}$.
[75] Cf. TW9, 21 A; 24.1,491$^{21-30}$.

"self-determination" of thinking that philosophy of nature arrives at a concrete conception of nature as a necessary unity.[76]

Hegel characterizes the philosophy of nature in a further way which can be seen as following from the task just laid out: It shall exhibit nature as a "living" and "purposive" unity.[77] Hegel credits ancient philosophers with having been cognizant of this task,[78] while it has largely been forgotten in modernity, before Kant and Schelling have reawoken it.[79] Hegel's wording should not be understood literally, though. Nature is neither a *living* organism nor is it a whole whose parts exist for the sake of the whole. What Hegel has in mind is rather that nature isn't an aggregate or an additive unity of independent items. Its fundamental features must rather be connected to one another essentially.[80] The unity of nature cannot be an additive one, and the form of explanation appropriate to it is thus teleological rather than mechanical, that is it does not proceed from parts to whole but from whole to parts. This does not contradict the possibility of explaining subordinate natural phenomena such as impact or adhesion mechanistically, that is by recourse to independently characterizable parts and external relations between them. It just means that the unity of nature on the whole defies mechanistic explanation.

Seen from the vantage point of spirit, cognition of nature is spirit's attempt to "find itself in nature".[81] This claim cannot be understood literally, for spirit is embodied *self-determination*, while nature is a realm of necessary and contingent *determinateness*. That spirit is said to find its essence, self-determination, in nature means that it acquires a concrete understanding of the essential unity of the physical universe *by way of self-determining thought*, namely, by immanently unfolding the inchoate concept of nature as self-externality, thereby arriving at *an evermore determinate* understanding of the kind of unity the physical universe exhibits. Rather than being alien to the self-determination of pure thinking, the necessary unity of nature can in fact only be brought into view by way of pure thinking. There is thus something about nature, namely, its essential unity, its form, which is akin to pure thought. It is in this sense that spirit engaging in philosophy of nature "finds itself" in nature.

In Hegel's system philosophy of nature is preceded by logic. Logic abstractly foreshadows philosophy of nature insofar as it has an ontological dimension, unfolding in pure thought the notion of being qua being. We thus know, for instance, that the logical forms that pertain to an objective world as such, that is mechanism, chemism, and teleology, must have counterparts in nature. The spatiotemporal continuum must accordingly have traits that can be known

---

[76] See 20,236$^{8-11}$. [77] 24.1,6$^{2-3}$; [78] See 24.1,6$^{4-13}$.
[79] See 24.1,131$^{19-21}$; 24.2,946$^{10-14}$; 24.2,955$^{19-22}$. [80] Cf. 24.1,6$^{32-35}$; 24.2,945$^{18-31}$.
[81] 24.1,205$^{3-5}$; 24.1,7$^{11-13}$; 24.2,938$^{12-13}$.

through these forms of thought. That logic develops forms of thought pertaining to the objective world as such does not mean that these forms are abstract entities which are somehow contained in nature. It rather means that the natural universe lends itself to articulation by way of these forms. However, the task of developing the concept of nature, even while it may be aided by recourse to *logical concepts*, cannot be facilitated by a *return* to *logical* insights which apparently anticipate nature. Philosophy of nature must unfold *immanently*, rather than appealing to *prior* logical insights in places where proceeding immanently seems difficult. Doing otherwise amounts to unduly conflating logic and philosophy of nature.

In distinction to Aristotle and Kant Hegel does not begin philosophy of nature with the concept of relatively self-standing items in nature, namely, bodies in motion, but with the most minimal concept of something real one can conceive of, namely, self-externality. The scientific concept corresponding to it is that of a continuum, as has already been indicated. As the very first concept of the philosophy of nature, *self-externality* is implicitly understood as *immediate* self-externality, namely, as the concept of a *coextensive* continuum, that is one that is given all at once, rather than a mediated continuum, that is one that isn't given all at once but successively. Self-externality, in other words, is at first conceived of as a spatial rather than a temporal continuum.

It has likewise been indicated that Hegel also characterizes nature, that is self-externality, by recourse to logical notions, designating it as the "idea in the form of otherness" or the "idea as being." However, these ways of approaching the concept of nature from the vantage point of logic do not entail that the concept of nature can be reduced to logical notions. It cannot, because these logical characterizations do their job of pointing to the concept of nature by way of misfiring, only: The logical idea is the thoroughly mediated system of internally related thought-determinations which do *not* stand to each other as something or other. In consequence, it cannot exhibit the "form of otherness" or "immediacy." Formulations that might appear as definitions of the concept of nature cast in logical terms, therefore merely point out the need to think a *counterpart* to the logical idea that shares its intelligibility while being marked by otherness and immediacy. Such hints at the concept of nature are only cashed in concretely by the idea of self-externality which is not itself a logical concept, but the first concept of the real sciences of philosophy or the first *real* concept, for short. Its being a non-logical or real concept does not prevent it from being a pure concept, that is one that has its source in mere thinking.

Pure real concepts are formally different from logical concepts insofar as they pertain to the unity of something that does not itself belong to the order of thought, namely, nature or reality as such. In consequence, transitions within the philosophy of nature have their own peculiar form which is different from transitions between logical concepts. The grounds of transitions in the philosophy of nature can be obscured in three ways: By conflating the concept of a trait of nature with that trait itself, by conflating the philosophical transition between two concepts of such traits with a real transition on the part of nature, and by taking recourse to a purely logical ground, that is one that would justify an analogous transition in logic, to account for a transition within the philosophy of nature. All these types of conflation amount to some sort of misguided logicism within the philosophy of nature. Unfortunately, such conflations do not just occur in certain readings of Hegel, but occasionally in Hegel himself, while he also warns against them.[82]

The first two types of logicism conflate the philosophical concept of a feature of nature with that very feature itself, and the transition between concepts with a real transition on the part of nature. A twofold conflation of that sort might *seem* to be at work in Hegel insofar as he doesn't distinguish, in most places, between features of nature such as space, or time, and their respective concepts, claiming, for instance, that "space itself passes over into time."[83] Commentators have remarked that this way of talking should be taken with a grain of salt, namely, as designating a transition on the level of concepts, for example from the concept of space to that of time.[84] However, Hegel cannot be exonerated that easily, because conceptual transitions in the philosophy of nature are transitions between concepts of something real. This inevitably raises the question of what corresponds to such a transition on the part of the real. Phrasing conceptual transitions as if they occurred on the part of nature itself conceals that this question needs to be asked, as we shall see more concretely below.

The third type of logicism is methodological rather than material: It motivates a transition between concepts of something real by recourse to a kind of reason that can only ground an analogous transition between logical concepts. To give an example: Trying to motivate the transition from the concept of a point to the concept of a line by recourse to the claim that the point is the "first negation" of space and that "negation" points beyond itself toward a "negation of negation," as Hegel as well as some commentators do, involves a logicist fallacy. It must be the real content of the concept of a point rather than mere logical reflection on this concept which motivates the transition from this concept to that of a line.[85]

Having pointed out possible confusions that can obscure conceptual transitions in the philosophy of nature we can now address what rationally motivates such transitions. Abstractly speaking, these transitions must be *immanent*, that is.

---

[82] Cf. 24.1,217$^{15\text{-}25}$. [83] 24.1,235$^{11\text{-}13}$; cf. 20,251^{23}; 24.1,227$^{6\text{-}8}$.
[84] Cf. Wandschneider 1982, 30. [85] Cf. Section 2.1.

motivated by the fact that the concept at hand is found insufficient *by its own standards*, rather than with regard to any external standard. Not all transitions from one concept to another are of the same sort. The insufficiency might very well be located on the conceptual level, insofar as a concept, for instance, that of a plant, is implicitly characterized in contrast to another concept, for example that of an animal. The concept of a plant points to that of an animal, because it is part of the concept of a plant that a plant grows in such a way that what accrues can as well exist as an independent plant. In consequence, the concept of a plant contains an in-built contrast to the concept of an organism which grows in such a way that what accrues *cannot* as well exist as an independent organism. In other words, the concept of an organic "dividual" points to the concept of an organic "individual." A transition of this sort is formally different from another kind of transition, namely, one that involves a real contradiction, which means that the real correlate of the concept is essentially unstable. Exhibiting a real contradiction as such motivates a transition to the concept of the real consequence of that instability, for example a transition from the concept of space to that of time, insofar as time is nothing but the manifestation of the instability pertaining to space.

While the aforementioned transitions take their point of departure from *one* concept, there is yet another type of transition which relies on there already being two concepts at hand, for instance the concepts of space and time. The transition to a third concept can be motivated by that these two concepts are as of yet *merely logically* conjoined while what they designate must have a real unity on the level of nature itself. A transition from space and time to motion, for instance, can be motivated by the insight that the *logical* conjunction that conjoins the concepts of space *and* time must have a *real* counterpart, that is that there must be something in which space and time have a *real* unity rather than one that is merely thought, that is motion. The transition from the concept of inert matter to that of heavy matter is in turn motivated by that motion cannot be related to matter by way of logical disjunction, only, as a property that matter *does or does not* have. For the connection between motion and matter to be a real one rather than one that is merely thought, matter must in itself contain a source of motion – an insight that yields the concept of heavy matter.

As these examples show, conceptual transitions in the philosophy of nature cannot as such be taken to signify a real transition on the part of nature itself. To get a clear grip on these transitions, it does not suffice to subscribe to Hegel's warning that such transitions do not as such signify a temporal process on the part of nature. It would be equally misguided to assume that the real correlates of such concepts "ground" further features of nature in an atemporal manner. The transition from space and time to motion, for instance, does not show that space and time "ground" motion. Only something that exists can ground something else. The conceptual transition from space and time to motion, however, makes explicit that space and time do not exist independently of motion. As features of the natural universe they must have a real connection among each other rather than one that is only thought, and motion is what they have their real connection in. The transition from the concepts of *space* and *time* to that of motion thus exhibits space and time as dependent on motion, rather than grounding it.

Concepts which have their proper place in the philosophy of nature exhibit a kind of unity that is formally different from that of logical concepts. Their notional unity, that is the way in which their marks are united in the concept, points to another kind of unity, namely, one between corresponding features of reality. On the one hand, a real unity can be such as to involve features that are dependent parts or moments of an overarching whole. This applies to space and time insofar as they are "forms"[86] of a universe marked by motion and rest. On the other hand, such features can be externally related to each other, for example motion and rest can *appear* as accidental states of inert matter. If features of nature have their real unity as moments of an overarching whole, the concept of that whole cannot have an additive unity, that is it cannot be reduced to the concepts of those features and some sort of logical connection between them.

The concepts of motion and rest, for instance, cannot involve the concept of place as a determinate mark that is independent of recourse to motion and rest. They must rather involve an understanding of place as spatial position defined in relation to something that is either in motion or at rest. The unity of the concept of motion thus isn't an additive one, that is it cannot be reduced to marks which do not involve recourse to motion and rest. A clear understanding of the irreducible non-additive unity of the concept of motion, for instance, can thus only be obtained through a certain way of arriving at it, namely, by exhibiting a view of place as independent of recourse to something at rest or in motion as imaginary.

Even while pure concepts of nature are formally different from logical concepts they presuppose logical concepts. For the concepts of fundamental traits of nature such as space, time, motion, and matter are developed, one after the other, by way of pure thinking. Subsequent concepts in this series result from that previous ones are found lacking in that they either involve a contradiction or a logical connection whose real correlate is as of yet undetermined. Diagnosing a contradiction involved in a real concept or asking for the real correlate of the mere logical connection between such

---

[86] Cf. 20,243^{20}–244^{6}.

concepts inevitably involves logical concepts and operations. Even while the concepts developed in Hegel's philosophy of nature aren't logical concepts, but real ones, the philosophy of nature is therefore nonetheless permeated by logical concepts: The concept of motion as a change of place mediated by a change of time, for instance, involves the logical concepts of *change* and *mediation*.

Hegel's philosophy of nature abounds with explanations of real concepts in terms of logical concepts or by recourse to logical concepts that characterize the position of the real concept within a series of such concepts. Examples of the former are Hegel's explanation of time as "the concept which is there" (*daseiender Begriff*[87]), of matter as "being-for-self which is there" (*daseiendes Fürsichsein*[88]) or light as "identity which is there" (*daseiende Identität*[89]). Examples of the latter are his characterization of the point as the first "negation of space,"[90] of the line as "the negation of the negation of space"[91] or of matter as the "immediate unity" of space and time.[92] It is important to be clear about the status of such statements: They do neither directly provide a real concept nor define it, but point to it indirectly by way of external reflection.

Explanations of the first sort do not provide or define the concept at issue, because they are *paradoxical* combinations of logical concepts: *Identity* and *the concept* are logical determinations that are *not* just *there*, but *essentially mediated*. Claiming, for instance, that time is the concept which is there or that light is identity which is there merely points out a certain *analogy* between these real concepts and those logical determinations, for nature as such neither contains self-determination nor identity. It remains somewhat unclear how Hegel comes up with these logical analogies. In any event, the order of logical concepts he takes recourse to in his philosophy of nature does not correspond to the order of these concepts in his *Logic*.

Characterizations of the second sort reflect on the conceptual path by which the notion at hand has been reached, referring back to concepts it sublates, while not concretely engaging with the content of the concept at issue. A contentful explanation of the notion of a *line* would rather exhibit it as the "spatiality of the point"[93] or as a spatial manifold whose principle and limit the point is.[94] While reflective explanations by recourse to *logical* concepts provide information about the position of one real concept in relation to others or elucidate it by way of analogy with logical concepts, explanations of the latter sort elucidate the concept at issue and thereby shed light on its scientific counterpart.

---

[87] $9,34^{20}$. [88] $TW9,60A; 21.4,545^{24-25}$. [89] $TW9,112A; 24.1,48^{18-19}$. [90] $20,245^{17}$.
[91] $20,245^{20}$. [92] $20,252^{11}$. [93] $20,245^{19}$. [94] See $20,245^{17-18}; 8,7^{8-24}$.

1.6 Approaches to Hegel's Philosophy of Nature

As indicated earlier, philosophy of nature in the distinctively modern sense was a "young discipline" in Hegel's day. The kind of philosophy of nature he devised was without precedent indeed. Philosophy of nature in his sense has turned out to be a short-lived enterprise insofar as there have not been any major works that can count as original continuations on the kind of inquiry into nature Hegel conceived, with the exception of the late Schelling's *Presentation of the Process of Nature*.[95] Even while there have been a few ambitious attempts at reconstruction which take Hegel's project of a philosophy of nature completely seriously, speculative philosophy of nature as a self-standing discipline seems to have died with Hegel. More generally, it is already in the mid-nineteenth century that philosophy of nature in the distinctively post-Kantian sense has largely been replaced by the much more modest endeavor of philosophy of science that does not seek to provide *independent* philosophical insight into nature by way of pure thinking, but rather reflects on the procedures of empirical science.

In light of the historical fate of speculative philosophy of nature it would neither be adequate to outright dismiss this kind of philosophical approach to nature as spurious nor to first and foremost blame an allegedly scientific posterity with sheer lack of comprehension. Taking the latter stance would render Hegelian philosophy of nature a disservice, because it precludes the *kind* of approach to nature Hegel devised from being taken seriously as a viable endeavor.

While scientistic criticism which Hegel's philosophy of nature has been subject to since the mid-nineteenth century has indeed been based on a distorted view of the nature of his endeavor, there are nonetheless flaws inherent to Hegel's philosophy of nature which have contributed to its falling into disrepute. Exhibiting a philosophical approach to nature of the sort Hegel devised as still viable today will therefore require acknowledging that the actual shape he gave to that enterprise is ambiguous. Hegel himself acknowledges this when remarking that it is particularly difficult to find "stable ground" in this part of philosophy.[96] Taking philosophy of nature in Hegel's sense seriously as a viable philosophical option requires to acknowledge at least three limitations that beset the shape Hegel has given to this project and to scrutinize the extent to which his concrete realization of that endeavor is affected by these limitations.

---

[95] SW10, 301–390. Cf. Martin 2025c for a typological comparison of this work with Hegel's philosophy of nature.
[96] 24.2,957$^{5-7}$.

First and foremost, Hegel's philosophy of nature is limited due to its historical situatedness in that it does not incorporate certain seemingly fundamental concepts of contemporary science such as *curvature*, *quanta*, *energy*, or *entropy*. Saying so much does not imply that all of these concepts could or should be incorporated into a philosophy of nature in Hegel's sense. It only means that those who view Hegel's philosophy of nature as a viable philosophical endeavor have to inquire whether his stance might be incoherent in places due to its not touching upon such concepts.

Second, Hegel's philosophy of nature is limited due to a certain bias on his part in favor of a mesoscopic approach to nature which seeks to stick closely to the everyday phenomenology of natural processes rather than delving deep into their microscopic or cosmological dimensions.[97] This does not mean that Hegel's philosophy of nature would not involve *theoretical* concepts such as that of gravity or magnetism. It rather means that Hegel abstains from asking questions which pertain to the microscopic structure of matter or to anything larger than the solar system let alone the overall shape of the physical universe. His reluctance to ask questions of the former sort might be due to his anti-atomist stance[98] which seems reasonable to the extent in which it is based on the rejection of empty space, while this doesn't entail that philosophy of nature should not engage with microscopic features of matter. Hegel's reluctance to address cosmological questions, on the other hand, might be due to him lacking the idea of a finite but unbounded universe, which leaves him with a view of the universe as an endless spatiotemporal recurrence of solar systems.

The third and most severe limitation of Hegel's philosophy of nature is methodological. Taking his endeavor seriously requires one to critically examine each step with an eye on whether it lives up to the internal standard of the endeavor, namely, that the transition from one concept to the other is required to account for the essential unity of nature. Many transitions might not live up to this standard. Some might have to be dismissed as logicist in the sense of projecting an abstract logical form onto a topic in the philosophy of nature, suggesting that a concrete understanding of that topic has been achieved, while, in fact, it hasn't. One might wonder, for instance, whether Hegel's account of four types of heavenly body[99] amounts to more than a *mere application* of the *logical* concept of *absolute mechanism* to certain *empirical* phenomena. One accordingly needs to critically evaluate to which extent a transition in Hegel's philosophy of nature can indeed count as a transition on the level of pure thought *of nature*, rather than amounting to a mere *blend* of *logical* and *empirical* concepts in face of a certain kind of natural phenomenon.

---

[97] Cf. Falkenburg 1993, 542. [98] See $20,134^{24}$–135^1; $24.2,943^{5\text{-}11}$. [99] See E§§274–80.

While there are a good number of historical studies of Hegel's philosophy,[100] others have engaged with it first and foremost on a metaphilosophical and methodological level.[101] However, the nature of Hegel's project as well as its limitations can ultimately only be assessed by way of argumentative reconstruction of the concrete path taken. Some readings which live up to this requirement seek to provide a reconstruction of Hegel's philosophy of nature *as it stands*, suggesting that later scientific achievements should be seen as both compatible with it and contingent, rather than potentially testifying of its fundamental incompleteness.[102] Other readers have tried to emend Hegel's account of nature in light of more recent scientific findings, which helps to reveal its contemporary relevance.[103] Such emendations might leave one wondering, though, to which extent they are philosophical or empirical in nature. Further readings seek to do away with the idea that philosophy of nature is supposed to achieve some sort of purely conceptual insight into nature, attributing it the meta-scientific task of exhibiting a certain kind of order between the sciences of nature, their concepts, and their methods.

The approach taken in this study deviates from the aforementioned ones in reconstructing Hegel's philosophy of nature as a rigorous nonempirical investigation of the concept of nature by way of pure thinking, an investigation that takes up and integrates certain scientific concepts, while not relying on scientific knowledge of nature.[104] The present reconstruction takes Hegel's claim to *philosophical* insight into nature seriously, while finding fault with a number of steps he took in the course of realizing that endeavor.

During the last years, systematic interest in Hegel's philosophy of nature has largely been focused on his conception of organic life.[105] The interest has both been sparked by a philosophical quest for "mind's place in nature" as well as ecological concerns. In the wake of John McDowell's reappropriation of the old distinction between first and second nature many have turned to Hegel's account of organic life in search of conceptual resources for a naturalistic conception of mind.[106] On the ensuing view, spirit or mindedness is the result of some sort of maturation or self-formation on the part of a certain kind of living being that is undisputedly part of nature. Views of this sort promise to

---

[100] Cf. Petry 1970; von Engelhardt 1976; Petry 1987; Petry 1993; Bonsiepen 1997. For a typological overview of paradigm shifts in the interpretation of Hegel's philosophy of nature see Ferrini 2014.
[101] Cf. for example Stone 2005;   [102] Cf. for example Houlgate 2006; Houlgate 2024.
[103] Cf. Winfield 2017; Winfield 2018; Stekeler 2023.
[104] Cf. Wandschneider 1982 as a precedent of this kind of approach.
[105] Cf. for example Spahn 2007; Sell 2014; Ng 2020.
[106] Cf. for example the pertinent contributions in Corti and Schülein 2022; Corti and Schülein 2023.

do away with an apparent dualism between mind and nature. However, this kind of approach to Hegel's philosophy of nature is problematic. It tends to bypass his conception of inorganic nature due to the assumption that inorganic nature belongs to the domain of science only. This assumption, however, bridges one gap at the expense of opening another insofar as it prevents us from arriving at a unified philosophical conception of nature as comprising both inorganic and organic nature. It moreover leads to a flat conception of organic nature, since it ignores Hegel's insight that the emergence of organic life necessarily presupposes all stages of inorganic nature dealt with beforehand. Organic life, as he seeks to show, cannot occur in any arbitrary corner of the universe, but only in the setting of a terrestrial planet comprising solid, liquid, and gaseous matter circulating under the impact of solar radiation. Merely focusing on Hegel's account of organic life thus makes one overlook what might be most profound about it, namely, his emphasis on the planetary dimension of life.

Finally, the whole suggestion that the idea of mind as second nature allows for a *naturalist* understanding of mind is fundamentally at odds with Hegel's clear-cut distinction between the philosophy of nature and the philosophy of spirit. That Hegel does not conceive of spirit as part of nature by no means implies that his distinction between them entails dualism. Even while spirit, on his account, is self-determining, while nature is a realm of determinate being, his philosophy of nature exhibits nature as a realm that allows to be transformed by self-determining activity so as to give rise to a shared world in which freedom is actual, while such self-determining activity presupposes organic embodiment, rather than occurring in a void. However, the first and foremost topic of Hegel's philosophy of nature is nature, rather than spirit. His subsequent account of spirit as self-determining activity that has a foothold in nature while not being part of nature can only be understood against the background of his philosophical conception of nature which is the topic of this study. Not only is Hegel's conception of spirit non-naturalist both in the sense of it not being part of nature as well as in the sense of spirit requiring other forms of cognition than nature does. His conception of nature is non-naturalist as well, insofar as it doesn't take its point of departure from a *given* understanding of nature but arrives at the concept of nature by way of pure thinking, for which reason that concept is based on a logical account of thought and being, rather than standing on its own.[107]

---

[107] Cf. Stein 2024 on the non-physicalist, non-naturalist, and anti-essentialist character of Hegel's conception of both nature and spirit.

2 *Mechanics*: Space, Time, Motion, and Heavy Matter

Hegel's conceptual investigation of nature is divided into *Mechanics*, *Physics*, and *Organic Physics*.[108] *Mechanics* envisages nature as fundamentally immediate or non-relational, while *Physics* views it as relational. Nature is fundamentally non-relational insofar as it can be viewed as homogenous. Viewed as homogeneous, the realm of externality does not involve specifically different parts within itself. *Mechanics* accordingly investigates global features of nature such as space, time, and motion, while also dealing with movable bulks of matter which it treats as homogenous. That *Mechanics* treats of externality as *fundamentally* non-relational is compatible with it envisaging *relations* between different kinds of body, such as the gravitational attraction between the sun and a planet, provided that the relata are *treated as homogenous or punctiform*. *Mechanics* thus provides conceptual foundations for the kinematics and dynamics of mass points.

Mechanics and *Physics* do not conceive of different kinds of matter, but take different perspectives on matter. Matter as viewed by *Mechanics* will turn out to be an abstraction: Envisaging bulks of matter as mass points in motion *presupposes* that such bulks are contiguous within themselves and that there are different kinds of matter. For if matter was *exactly* alike *everywhere*, it would hang together in the same way ubiquitously and thus couldn't move, provided that motion consists in matter changing its location with regard to other matter. What accounts for the inner contiguity of a bulk of matter are *polar* forces. *Physics* accordingly envisages bulks of matter as essentially relational and thus inhomogeneous in themselves. The interactions it treats of are hence *specific* interactions between *specific* bulks of matter, rather than *universal* interactions between bulks of matter in general. *Physics* thus crucially deals with electromagnetic and chemical properties of matter.

Organic Physics envisages externality neither as fundamentally non-relational nor as involving relations between different relata, but as in relation to itself. Nature, however, insofar as it is a realm of externality or otherness, does not literally comprise anything that relates to itself such as self-conscious thinking does. That *Organic Physics* treats of externality insofar as it stands in a relation to itself rather means that it deals with bulks of matter that are internally articulated in such a way that their parts are what they are in virtue of their contribution to the existence of the whole by way of mutual interaction with other kinds of part. *Organic Physics* thus envisages nature insofar as it requires a teleological form of explanation. The relation between *Organic Physics* and the previous two parts is not as straightforward as the relation

---

[108] See 20,252–253.

between these two among each other. It raises the question whether it is a contingent fact that there is organic nature beyond inorganic nature. This question would have to be answered by recourse to the concept of inorganic nature rather than by recourse to metaphysical or empirical assumptions.[109]

Mechanics is divided into a first part, entitled *Space and Time*, which deals with *global* features of nature, that is those which characterize the natural universe ubiquitously, rather than just *locally*, namely, spatiality, temporality, and, as it turns out, motion and matter. Against this background, *Finite Mechanics* zooms in on relations between finite bulks of matter in motion interacting with one another. By way of conclusion, *Absolute Mechanics* marries the concern with *global unity* with that for *local relations* between *different* bodies impacting on each another by envisaging a *system of bodies in motion* which is *absolute* in that these motions aren't externally conditioned but express the nature of matter in a self-contained way. The transition from *Finite* to *Absolute Mechanics* thereby reveals motion to have a source in the nature of matter and thus exhibits gravitational motion as the motion of matter as such. It should be noted that *Absolute Mechanics* leaves things at a *local* level, focusing on solar systems, while not seeking to philosophically address the *global* unity of the physical universe. Hegel in fact dismisses the idea that there could be a philosophical *cosmology*.[110] In absence of compelling reasons for this, this dismissal might be seen as reflecting the fact that scientific cosmology was still in its infancy during Hegel's times.

2.1 Space and Time

Most fundamentally, nature is a "realm of self-externality" (*Sphäre des Außersichseins*).[111] This means that nature is, primarily, a manifold whose elements or parts do not have any determination exclusively for themselves. What is comprised in this manifold is accordingly such that by being what it is it already points beyond itself. An element of that sort thus lacks proper determinacy of its own that is independent of its surroundings. By being what it is, it is at the same time already beyond itself, that is it is transient into its environment. Insofar as the fundamental character of nature is self-externality, nature is a manifold that does not consist of a determinate number of independent parts or elements, that is a continuum.[112] A continuum is a manifold that does not require any sort of unification on top of the unity pertaining to the manifold as

---

[109] Lack of space prevents me from giving a detailed account of *Organic Physics* and its relations to the two previous parts of Hegel's *Philosophy of Nature* in this Element. I provide a comprehensive treatment elsewhere, see fn. 204.
[110] Cf. TW9,81-82A.; 24.1,31$^{18\text{-}22}$; 24.1,283$^{2\text{-}4}$. [111] 20,247$^{8\text{-}10}$; cf. 20,237$^{3\text{-}7}$; 20,243$^{15\text{-}17}$.
[112] Cf. 20,243$^{17\text{-}19}$; 20,244$^{6\text{-}10}$.

such. A simple part that can be singled out from a continuum, that is a point, is in and by itself already beyond itself and, hence, integrated into a larger whole that surpasses it – a neighborhood, that is something that is closer to a given point than any point could be.

That nature in the sense of a realm that is inexhaustible by thought while not comprising anything unintelligible must have the character of a continuum can be seen as follows: What is inexhaustible by thought must be such as to *allow* for a multiplicity of items that are exactly alike to occur, that is it must allow for difference without distinguishability. For items which are qualitatively identical but numerically different cannot be distinguished by recourse to pure thought alone, but can be kept apart indexically, only, that is on condition that the keeping apart is achieved from a vantage point amid of what is being kept apart.

Absent any further considerations the continuum is at first envisaged as immediate or determined all at once, that is as a coextensive continuum: space.[113] Qua continuum space is a manifold that does not consist of a determinate number of distinct items. However, qua manifold it must allow to distinguish something within it,[114] and qua real it must allow for real distinctions, that is ones which are not merely drawn in thought. Since the nature of the spatial manifold has not been further specified apart from its being coextensive, the concept of space does not immediately point to any specific kind of manifold or subsection that might be distinguished within space. However, its being a *manifold* implies that it must allow distinguishing something within it that is not itself a manifold, but *simple*. The concept of space thus points to the concept of something simple that can be distinguished within it, that is the concept of a point.[115] Since a continuum does not consist of a determinate number of distinct items, space does not consist of points.[116] It rather comprises them in the sense of allowing points to be singled out. The concept of a point determinately negates the concept of space insofar as it is the concept of something unextended and thus non-spatial that is essentially related to space.

The relation between point and space must be a real one, that is one that is not only thought. On the face of it, it simply consists in points being "in" space. However, the apparently innocent claim that points are "in" space conceals

---

[113] Cf. 20,243$^{15\text{-}17}$. [114] Cf. 24.1,15$^{17\text{-}22}$. [115] Cf. 20,245$^{14\text{-}16}$.
[116] See 20,233$^{12\text{-}13}$; 20,244$^{6\text{-}10}$. Kauffman and Yeomans reconstruct Hegel's view of space in terms of transfinite set theory (cf. 2023, 103–4) which conceives of a continuous manifold as a particular kind of discrete manifold, a transfinite one. Attributing a view of this sort to Hegel seems both philologically and systematically inappropriate as it undermines his distinction between the logical and the real. For historical and systematic considerations on the irreducibility of continuous manifolds, see Wieland 1992, 278–315; Prauss 2017; Martin 2020a, 241–264; Martin 2020b.

a difficulty, namely, that points are conceived of as both unextended *and* essentially related to what is extended.[117] Instead of *merely logically* conjoining these features, one needs to ask what their *real* unity consists in. In other words, one needs to bring into view how a point is related to the extension surrounding it *by virtue of its way of being unextended*. Hegel's characterization of space as immediate *self-externality* provides a hint: A point must be conceived of as something which *on its own* smoothly *extends* into what it is not, its neighborhood. The neat separation between a point and its neighborhood is accordingly one that is drawn in thinking, only.

The insight that it belongs to the point to extend beyond itself gives rise to the notion of a dimension.[118] Dimensions are *independent* ways in which a point smoothly extends beyond itself into space. Since the space surrounding a point is a manifold that does not consist of a determinate number of parts, there must be indeterminately many ways in which a point smoothly extends beyond itself into space. Space can nevertheless comprise a determinate number of dimensions insofar as dimensions qua *independent* directions in space allow defining an *indeterminate* number of *derivative* directions by way of weighed combination.

Hegel seeks to prove that space must have three dimensions.[119] Attempts of this sort can fall prey to two kinds of fallacy: a logicist and a realist one. The logicist fallacy consists in arguing for three-dimensionality based on *logical* considerations. It might for instance be argued that the determinate negation of a concept is externally opposed to what it negates and therefore points beyond itself to double negation which must exhibit some sort of reflexivity rather than likewise being externally opposed to what it negates. By this criterion the line and the plane are then found lacking as candidates for the negation of the negation of space insofar as they interrupt or delimit space and are thus opposed to it instead of being fully spatial.[120] Not only does this argument unduly rely on abstract *logical* machinery instead of *immanently* unfolding the concept of space. The argument is moreover question-begging in that it implicitly presupposes that space is three-dimensional. For the line and the plane are coextensive continuous manifolds indeed which can only be found lacking *if viewed* against the background of *three-dimensional* space. Stripped off the logical machinery, the same sort of petitio is at work in young Hegel's argument that the point, the line, and the plane cannot stand on their own, but are mere limits of space insofar as the spatial relations between instances of each kind of geometrical object consist in a geometrical object of a higher rather than the same dimension.[121] Points are spatially connected by the line, lines by the plane,

---

[117] Cf. $24.1,228^{10\text{-}19}$. [118] Cf. $20,244^{20\text{-}22}$. [119] $20,246^{14\text{-}25}$.
[120] See Houlgate 2006, 124–125 with regard to E§245. [121] See $2,378^{4\text{-}12}$.

and planes by three-dimensional space, while disjoint three-dimensional spaces are connected by three-dimensional space. This argument won't do, however, because it presupposes that space is at least two- or three-dimensional. For only in that case does the question of the nature of the spatial connection between lines or planes even arise.

A proof of the three-dimensionality of space can only succeed, if three-dimensional space isn't implicitly taken as the measure in relation to which lines and planes are found lacking. The proof must rather envisage the line or the plane as candidates for space proper, that is as a space which can stand on its own, and it must then exhibit them as lacking *on their own terms* rather than in comparison with three-dimensional space. The inner deficiency of the line and the plane can only consist in their not allowing understanding their relation to the point as a fully real one, that is one that does not involve features which are merely thought. What this criterion concretely amounts to can best be seen when asking for what *really* relates a point to the surrounding space of hitherto unknown dimensionality.[122]

The relation between a point and the surrounding space must be real, that is spatial,[123] rather than merely thought. Claiming that it is the spatial environment into which the point is embedded which provides for the real relation between point and space is insufficient, both because the determinate nature of this environment is thereby left undetermined, and, more fundamentally, because the relationship between point and space must be a real one both ways, that is it must be possible to view it as proceeding from the point, rather than from the surrounding space, only. That the real relation between the point and space must be viewed as one that has its origin in the point means that the point must be both the principle and the limit of a spatial manifold.[124] A continuous manifold constituted and limited by the point is a line. Asking for the real relation between the point and its spatial environment of hitherto unknown dimension thus gives rise to the concept of a line, that is a one-dimensional continuous manifold.

In order to find out whether space could be just that, a one-dimensional manifold, it must be asked whether there is something lacking in the way in which a point relates to the line it is part of. To be self-sufficiently embedded into a continuous manifold surrounding it, the point must be seamlessly connected to its environment. *Seamless* connection to its environment requires that the point is not merely connected to that environment by a *determinate number* of "exits" into it, but that the manifold of its exits into space is itself a continuous rather than a discrete one. However, a point on a line exhibits only two exits into

---

[122] Cf. 24.1,16$^{25\text{-}28}$.   [123] Cf. 20,245$^{27\text{-}28}$.   [124] See 20.245$^{17\text{-}19}$; 24.1,17$^{1\text{-}3}$.

the linear manifold into which it is embedded,[125] that is the manifold of its seamless connections with the line is a discrete rather than a continuous one. The line accordingly isn't a self-sufficient space, because it doesn't allow for the manifold of relations between the point and itself to be fully real, that is a continuous manifold. The line must therefore be the principle and limit of a more encompassing spatial manifold which allows for the relation between the point and space to be fully real. The spatial manifold that is constituted by the line as both its principle and limit is the plane. The plane indeed lives up to the requirement that the manifold of exits of a point embedded into it is a continuous rather than a discrete manifold, namely, the numerically indeterminate manifold that can geometrically be represented by lines in a plane intersecting in this point.

It might thus seem that space does not have to have more than two dimensions, since the plane lives up to the criterion of allowing for the connection of the point to it to be fully real. However, based on the concepts of a point, a line, and a plane, further concepts can be defined by recourse to which it can be shown that the way in which the point is embedded into the plane isn't fully real nonetheless. These concepts are those of a direction and an angle. Based on them the concept of a direction C that is perpendicular to two perpendicular directions A and B can be formed. Nothing real corresponds to this concept, if space is in fact two-dimensional, that is this concept is empty in that case. However, the empty concept of a direction C which stands orthogonal to possible directions within the plane, allows showing that the way in which the point is embedded into the plane isn't fully real: It allows demarcating a respect in which such a point is not seamlessly embedded into a continuous manifold. That there is no direction C along which a point is seamlessly embedded into a surrounding manifold means that there is something about the point of the plane which prevents its relation to the surrounding space from being fully real, namely, a respect in which it isn't seamlessly embedded into a continuous manifold. In other words, the *flatness* of the plane brings with it a respect which defies its being a *self-contained* continuum.

Space must therefore be at least three-dimensional, for three-dimensional space surrounds the point in such a way that it isn't possible to demarcate by recourse to the concepts of a point, a line, and a plane respects in which a point in three-dimensional space isn't seamlessly embedded into a continuous manifold surrounding it.

---

[125] Cf. Wandschneider 1982, 57.

One might wonder, though, whether one cannot show by way of an analogous argument that space must be more than three-dimensional. *If* space is four-dimensional, it is indeed possible to indicate respects in which a point in three-dimensional space lacks a surrounding into which it is seemlessly embedded. However, this case crucially differs from the way in which two-dimensional space is found lacking. While a point in two-dimensional space is *unconditionally* lacking in that it exhibits certain respects in which it does not seemlessly extend beyond itself into a manifold surrounding it, a point in three-space could only be found to be lacking in this way *on condition* that space is in fact of higher dimensionality. We can conclude that physical space must *at least* be three-dimensional. It might not be decidable by way of a priori reflection whether it comprises even more dimensions.

Having characterized physical space, we can now address the question whether space could be all there is to nature, that is whether space could stand on its own. It will be shown that it cannot, due to its involving a real contradiction.[126] That the coextensive continuum involves a real contradiction is implicit in its characterization as a *manifold* that does not consist of a determinate number of items. Accordingly, the continuum is introduced as a multiplicity while at the same time being denied the status of a multiplicity.[127] Recourse to a multiplicity of elements is necessary to distinguish the continuum from what is absolutely simple, while such recourse is at the same time ruled out by its not consisting in a number of determinate elements.

One might object that the supposed contradiction can easily be avoided, if one abstains from characterizing the continuum by recourse to elements which it indeed isn't composed of, rather characterizing it as not consisting of determine items, while being infinitely divisible, the latter feature distinguishing it from what is utterly simple. However, recourse to infinite divisibility can't be the last word. For, infinite divisibility is a *possibility* which must have a foothold in the *actual* constitution of the continuum. Recourse to the possibility of infinite division thus raises the question for the actual feature of the continuum in which it is grounded. This feature cannot but consist in its involving a multiplicity. Recourse to a multiplicity of elements as well as the denial that the continuum consists of such elements are thus *both* ineliminable marks of the concept of space.

Even if a spatial continuum does not consist of distinct components and is thus a whole without parts, the only way to distinguish it from what is absolutely simple is by recourse to "virtual" parts. Accordingly, to get hold of the

---

[126] On the Hegelian notion of real contradiction in contrast to Kant's concept of real opposition cf. Martin 2025b.
[127] See TW9,42-43A.

continuum in thought, one cannot do without distinguishing something within it that is thereby posited as relatively independent, while having to immediately add that what is thus distinguished does not have a standing of its own and is thus absolutely dependent. To the extent that this characterization is appropriate to its subject matter, space itself is determined in a contradictory manner.[128]

That the concept of space involves a real contradiction neither means that there cannot be such a thing as space nor that space has to "pass over" into *something else*. Hegel's claim that space, on account of its contradictory nature, "passes over into time"[129] is not to be taken literally. The real contradiction pertaining to space rather entails that a certain restlessness *belongs to* space on account of a tension inherent to it. There is accordingly a passing away that is inherent to space. This passing away can neither consist in space vanishing into nothingness nor morphing into something non-spatial. Space cannot become something else, because change presupposes something undergoing it while staying the same. Given that space is a totality, if it were to become non-spatial there would be nothing left to undergo that change. A supposed change of space into something non-spatial would thus amount to the disappearance of space and the groundless emergence of something else. What the vanishing of space would leave us with is nothing, and nothing isn't a real but a logical determination, for nothing doesn't allow for difference without distinguishability. Accordingly, the restlessness of space that pertains to space on account of its contradictory nature can only consist in space constantly passing away *while also enduring*, that is in its passing away without being done away with for good.

Time is nothing other than the constant passing away that belongs to space essentially.[130] Accordingly, it is not a further independent feature of nature beyond space, but the constant manifestation of the restlessness belonging to space.[131] The concept of time thus amounts to the determinate negation of the concept of space, which means that it results from a real contradiction on account of which the concept of space points beyond itself. Insofar as time is the constant passing away inherent to space, time must likewise be a continuum,[132] albeit a successive, rather than a coextensive one. One might as well say that time is the mediated and mediating dimension of the immediate self-externality which space consists in.

Time is the doing away that belongs to space. While space is the inclusive side of self-externality, time is its exclusive side, the "negative unity of self-externality"[133] as Hegel put's it. As such it is likewise a continuous manifold,

---

[128] See 20,251$^{21\text{-}23}$.   [129] 20,251^{23}.   [130] Cf. TW9,48A.
[131] Cf. 20,247$^{7\text{-}11}$; 24.1,245$^{29\text{-}31}$.   [132] See 20,248$^{1\text{-}3}$.   [133] 20,247^{13}.

but its continuity does not consist in the seamless connection of something and other, but in the seamless self-replacement of something by something else. Time is thus that about the real which makes it "not be in virtue of being, and be in virtue of not-being."[134] That non-being is said to give rise to being might only appear contradictory as long as non-being is conceived of as subsisting independently, rather than as a dependent aspect of the real. That reality is temporal means that what is real is as such both on the verge of ceasing to exist as well as pregnant with what as of yet isn't. What as of yet isn't can only be real insofar as it is *infinitesimally* contained in what presently is: What *is* continuously transgresses itself and thus involves a certain direction beyond itself, even while not discretely incorporating anything that as of yet isn't. Physical time thus comprises past, present and future as dependent aspects of a continuous manifold: What *presently* is is on the verge of *being no more* in virtue of being about to actualize *what as of yet isn't*. Since nature is a continuous manifold, *in nature* the past and the present do not subsist in separation from the present and do not have discrete determinacy on their own.[135] They only have *infinitesimal* subsistence as the two ways in which the present continuously points beyond itself. This can best be illustrated by recourse to motion insofar as motion does not just involve something being here just now, but consists in something's being here just now in a way that involves a twofold directedness, namely, a direction in which it can no longer be found and one pointing to where it is about to be.

Time resolves the inner tension of space, namely, that of involving parts or elements, while not giving them any actual standing of their own, leaving them wholly virtual instead. By way of its successive nature time provides the point with actuality insofar as it is singled out as the present, while at the same time manifesting it to be null and void, as continuously slipping away.[136]

Spatial dimensions had been explained as *independent* ways in which a point can smoothly extend beyond itself, ways which can then be combined to define indeterminately many further derivative ways of extending beyond itself. Since time is the doing away inherent to space on the whole, it does not allow for multiple dimensions, that is for multiple *independent* ways of the present transcending itself.[137] Properly speaking, time does not even allow for one *dimension* in the sense of what allows for a *reversible* transition, for time can only pass. Present, past, and future cannot count as *dimensions* of time, because

---

[134] 20,247$^{14\text{-}15}$.

[135] Cf. 20,249$^{13\text{-}19}$. It is only on the level of spirit that past and future acquire a determinacy that is potentially discontinuous with the present, rather than being its infinitesimal temporal environment.

[136] See TW9,48A.   [137] Cf. 24.1,19$^{10\text{-}13}$.

they all pertain to the way in which a temporal point, a moment, seamlessly extends beyond itself, rather than to independent ways of so doing.[138]

It has been argued that space involves a real contradiction, a tension in virtue of which it constantly passes away while also enduring. The constant passing away of space is time, and time thus isn't a further global trait of nature added on top of space but rather one that is rooted in and necessitated by the nature of space itself. However, since nature is characterized by externality or otherness, space and time enjoy a *certain* independence of one another which allows one to deal with one without thereby dealing with the other. Space and time, the coextensive and the successive continuum, can indeed *appear* as juxtaposed, and one can indeed envisage the concept of space in abstraction from the concept of time, and vice versa. However, as global traits of nature, space and time, cannot *just* be juxtaposed. In other words, their unity or that on account of which they are global traits of one and the same universe cannot merely belong to the order of thought. It is therefore insufficient, if not misleading, to state that nature is both spatial *and* temporal, as has already been indicated. A universe that is both spatial and temporal can thus only be a *universe*, if there is another trait of nature of which space and time are dependent aspects. Insofar as nature is marked by externality, the feature of nature thanks to which space and time, rather than falling apart, are aspects of one and the same universe, will, on account of nature's otherness or externality, appear as external to both space and time, that is as something additional to them rather than as what they have their real unity in.

2.2 Motion and Matter

Since both space and time are features of nature, they must have a real connection rather than one that is merely thought.[139] Accordingly, the passage of time cannot be external to space, that is it must be concretely tied to what is *in* space rather being externally appended to space on the whole. This insight gives raise to what Hegel calls "place," that is a point in time tied to a point in space.[140] Time accordingly passes *somewhere* rather than *nowhere*, that is time is essentially local time. Its locality notwithstanding, time passes everywhere, that is any point in space is tied to the passage of time.

The concept of place is only a first step on the way to grasping the real connection of space and time. It is just the concept of something comprising both a point in space *and* a moment of time. The unity of a point in space *and* a moment of time can only be a real one, if the passing away that is characteristic of the moment is conceived of as *internal* to the point in space rather than

---

[138] Cf. 20,249$^{1\text{-}9}$.   [139] Cf. Houlgate 2006, 130.   [140] See 20,251$^{20\text{-}29}$.

logically conjoined with it. We have thereby arrived at the concept of a place going beyond itself, that is the concept of motion.[141] Motion indeed consists in a continuous change of *place* in Hegel's sense, that is in leaving behind an immediate pairing of a point in space and a point in time. It is thus only by way of motion that time and space have a *real* unity, and motion must thus be a ubiquitous and necessary trait of nature rather than an accidental and local one.

Motion presupposes something that moves. For a change of position is only possible between spatial positions which stay the same. *Real* motion therefore cannot amount to the motion of a point or a mere subsection of space. Motion thus presupposes something that is not itself a position in space, but something that fills space, that is matter.[142] The concept of motion thus points beyond itself to the concept of matter. Since motion must be actual, matter must be distributed inhomogeneously in space, for only on that condition can matter disentangle itself from its surroundings.

As change of position motion presupposes something with regard to which the thing in motion changes its position, that is something which is at rest in relation to that thing – a frame of reference, in modern parlance. The frame of reference in relation to which something is in motion cannot be space or a position in space. For space and time cannot have a real unity in certain regions of the universe, only, namely, ones filled with matter in motion. Consequently, a section of the universe which is at rest in relation to something that moves must as well involve a real unity between space and time, that is motion. Since motion presupposes matter, a frame of reference must thus itself be something material.

Given that a material system A which is at rest with regard to another moving system B must likewise be a moving system in relation to a system at rest, it follows that the moving system B can as well count as the frame of reference with regard to which the system A is in motion. Rest and motion are thus relative: Anything material that can be considered to be at rest can as well be considered to be in motion. In this way, Hegel's philosophy of nature allows to justify the Galilean principle of the relativity of motion and rest.[143]

---

[141] $20,261^{1-10}$. Motion is a direct variation of space with time. The real unity of time and space cannot consist in a direct variation of time with space, that is in time passing differently in different places. This would be at odds with the continuous nature of time, because it would preclude a continuous transition between local times by way of continuous transitions in space. Local times would rather vary in a discontinuous manner: they would be out of joint. The real unity between space and time must therefore, in the first instance, consist in a variation of space depending on the passage of time. That time cannot pass differently depending on where it passes is compatible with it passing differently depending on the state of motion; cf. Section 2.5.

[142] See TW9, 60A; $20,252^{10-12}$.

[143] See $24.1,293^{1}-30^{5}$. So far, motion has been introduced as just being there, rather than being caused, that is it is implicitly taken to be unaccelerated, that is inertial motion.

Hegel has shown space and time to be relative, too: They have proven to not subsist on their own, but to be essentially tied to matter in motion which their real connection consists in.[144] Consequently, neither is space a container that could as well be empty,[145] nor is time some sort of a flow that sweeps away things which happen to find themselves in it.[146] The passage of time is thus essentially tied to the motion of matter through space, rather than occurring independently of it.

Motion involves something's leaving the place it hitherto occupied, and it must thus be possible to draw a real distinction between a place and what it is filled with at a time – matter. Matter must be extended rather than punctiform for the following reason: Motion presupposes a real distinction between spatial position and something movable at that position. A point, however, is simple. Due to its simplicity it doesn't allow for a real distinction between spatial position and something filling it. Therefore, a point cannot *really* move and the motion of a point is something imaginary or *merely* thought, while what underlies real motion must be extended.

The way in which matter occupies a space must be different from the way a geometrical body does. Geometrical bodies are just sections of space which have been singled out by some intellectual operation. Hegel follows Kant in this regard who insists that matter "fills" (*erfüllen*) space rather than merely "occupying" (*einnehmen*) it.[147] A first step toward distinguishing space-filling from the mere occupation of space is that space-filling entails impenetrability in the sense of resistance to the intrusion of further matter into a space that is already filled with matter.[148] We cannot content ourselves with an explication of space-filling in terms of impenetrability, however, because impenetrability is a *dispositional* property specifying how matter that fills a certain space *would* react *if* other matter sought to intrude into it.[149] This leaves open what the underlying *actuality* of space-filling in which impenetrability has its ground consists in.[150]

Characterizing matter as extended, movable and impenetrable, provides us with "predicates" *proper* to matter,[151] while only yielding a preliminary conception of matter itself, because the first feature isn't peculiar to matter, while the others are mere dispositions of it which must have their ground in the *actual* constitution of matter.

Without much ado Hegel aligns himself with Kant's dynamical account of matter,[152] while mostly busying himself with reproaching Kant's way of

---

[144] Cf. 24.1,248^{22}–249^{2};TW9,59A.   [145] See 20,244$^{2-6}$.
[146] See 20,248$^{4-11}$; TW9,50A.; 24.1,287$^{14-18}$; 24.2,1009$^{9-28}$.
[147] AA4,497$^{2-13}$. Cf. 24.1,548^{26}.   [148] See AA4,496$^{16-19}$; 20,252$^{27-28}$.   [149] See AA4,496$^{7-9}$.
[150] Cf. AA4,496$^{19-20}$.   [151] 20,252$^{22-31}$.   [152] Cf. 20,254$^{14-18}$.

spelling it out with incoherence.[153] Before assessing Hegel's criticism of the specificities of Kant's dynamical account of matter in terms of attractive and repulsive forces, the reasons for the general idea that the essence of matter is force which both share in need to be explained. Hegel's reasoning on this topic is logicist in the sense that he characterizes matter by recourse to the notions of *being-for-self* (*Fürsichsein*) and *individuality* (*Vereinzelung*),[154] which are shown, in his *Logic*, to lead to the concept of a multiplicity of "ones" attracting and repulsing each other.[155] He thus imports a piece of abstract logical reasoning into his philosophy of nature which is insufficient as an answer to a question that arises with regard to matter, namely, how the *actual* constitution of matter underlying its impenetrability and mobility should be understood.

Kant, on the other hand, provides us with an argument for the dynamical conception of matter which indeed falls into the domain of philosophy of nature proper, relying on his distinction between logical and real ground. In order to show what space-filling really consists in, Kant reduces to absurdity the competing logicist view according to which the features we have already attributed to matter, its being extended and impenetrable, provide us with a sufficient conception of matter that could stand on its own. According to the logicist view, the property of space-filling can be reduced to the property of occupying a space (which geometrical and material bodies are thought to share) and the property of being impenetrable or "solid" (which is thought to be distinctive of material bodies).[156] On this account, something fills space, iff it occupies that space *and* is solid.

Kant objects to this view that there must be a *real* connection between occupation of a space and impenetrability rather than the two being *merely logically conjoined*: It does not suffice to say that it belongs to the *concept* of matter to resist intrusion by other matter, for matter cannot resist intrusion *merely in virtue of the law of non-contradiction*, that is insofar as such intrusion would contradict what is contained in the concept of matter.[157] It would rather have to be shown that impenetrability has a *real foothold* in the way in which matter occupies space[158]. For this reason a conception of matter that merely juxtaposes the two features of extension and impenetrability is found lacking. It is therefore wrong to assume that geometrical bodies and material bodies occupy space in the same way, while material bodies exhibit the extra feature of not just occupying space but being impenetrable as well. Instead, occupation with regard to geometrical bodies means that such bodies are subsections of the spatial continuum which have been arbitrarily singled out by some intellectual

---

[153] Cf. 20,254$^{18\text{-}23}$. [154] See 20,254$^{5\text{-}8}$. [155] See 20,134^{1}–135^{12}. [156] See AA4,497$^{30\text{-}33}$.
[157] See AA4,497^{33}–498^{5}. [158] Cf. AA4,498$^{5\text{-}9}$.

operation and aren't real, accordingly, while occupation of space with regard to material bodies must mean something real. For the very same reason an opponent to the dynamical account of matter can't withdraw to claiming that space-filling simply consists in occupying a space in an "impenetrable" or "solid way" which allegedly cannot be explained any further. This won't do, because it is a category mistake to appeal to the geometrical concept of occupation when what is at issue is how matter is "in" space, and because impenetrability is merely the potential to resist other matter on condition that the latter seeks to intrude into a space already taken, while this leaves open the question for the actuality in which that potential has its ground.

Qua dispositional property impenetrability must have a foothold in the actual constitution of matter and can therefore only be a derivative feature proper to matter, rather than being its essence. The nature of matter must hence consist in *actual* activity that is both spatially located and directed, because only on that condition will it keep other matter at bay.[159] Insofar as force is real activity that is both spatially located and directed, that is activity expanding through space, the essence of matter has thus been exhibited as force.

It is important, though, as Hegel keeps insisting, to not conceive of the force which matter consists in in merely reflective terms, that is to not distinguish between the "force itself" and its "expression" or actualization.[160] The force which matter consists in is something actual, rather than a mere disposition. Hegel takes the term "force" to suggest this latter understanding and therefore rejects it, even while subscribing to a dynamical account of matter.

Kant himself concretizes his dynamical conception of matter by the following line of thought which is usually referred to as the "balancing argument".[161] Obviously, the force underlying impenetrability must be a repelling rather than an attracting one. Even while it has its origin in a point, the activity of a repelling force must extend through space, because matter isn't punctiform. In consequence, if the force of matter was merely repelling, matter would be infinitely dispersed, because any punctiform center of force would repel the others. Therefore, space could in fact not be *filled* with matter, which is absurd. Accordingly, instead of merely consisting in a repelling force, matter must be constituted by an attracting force as well. These two forces must be balanced: Attraction holds matter together against the repelling tendency to infinitely disperse, and repulsion keeps matter from imploding into a mere point due to its inherent attraction. Kant recognizes that attracting and repelling forces cannot act in the same way while just differing in direction, because in this case their net sum would everywhere be zero which is at odds with matter being

---

[159] Cf. AA4,497$^{24\text{-}28}$; TW9, 64 A; 24.2,548$^{25\text{-}28}$.   [160] 20,253$^{17\text{-}30}$.   [161] Cf. Warren 2010.

impenetrable. The ways in which attraction and repulsion reach out through space must thus be different, repulsion proximally prevailing over attraction so as to prevent implosion, and attraction distally prevailing over repulsion so as to prevent complete dispersal.

Schelling was the first to find fault with Kant's conception of matter as consisting in both attracting and a repelling forces,[162] and Hegel follows him in that regard. Schelling's original criticism concerns the specific way in which Kant thought repelling and attracting forces to act, namely, his idea that repulsion is a contact force, acting only in the plane in which bodies touch. This idea, however, undermines Kant's dynamical account of matter, because the concept of contact presupposes that of material bodies and therefore cannot be used in an explanation of what constitutes a material body. Even while Kant is right to subscribe to an account of matter as *constituted* by forces, his specific way of spelling this idea out turns force into a mere property inherent to a bulk of matter.

More fundamentally, Hegel objects to Kant's dynamical account of matter that he conceives of repulsive and attractive force as two independent forces,[163] thereby missing matter's real unity.[164] This criticism might seem surprising given that Kant's balancing argument reduces the independent occurrence of any of these two to absurdity, showing that one force of matter as such cannot occur without the other. However, Hegel might say that the balancing argument comes too late, because repulsive and attractive force are *at first* characterized independently of one another, while it is only in a second step that Kant shows that they cannot in fact occur this way. This, however, leaves us with the task to conceive of them as moments or dependent aspects of a "totality," rather than "self-standing"[165] forces. Instead of relying on a *counterfactual* and hence *unreal* scenario concerning matter *taken in isolation* which is what Kant's balancing argument does, Hegel therefore seeks to develop a *concrete* understanding of the repulsive and attractive *moments* of matter.[166]

2.3 *Finite Mechanics*: Inertia, Impact, and Free Fall

If time and space are *global* features of nature and if motion is what space and time have their real unity in, while motion presupposes matter, matter must be a plenum, that is fill space *ubiquitously*, rather than in a gappy way.[167] On the other hand, matter must be distributed unevenly, because only on that condition can bulks of matter be separated from other bulks of matter which is what

---

[162] Cf. Förster 2022, 171–192. [163] See 20,254$^{18\text{-}22}$. [164] See 20,254^{24}–255^2.
[165] 20,254^{27}. [166] Cf. 20,254$^{5\text{-}10}$. [167] Cf. 24,1,546^{25}–547^2.

motion requires. *Finite Mechanics* unfolds how a finite bulk of matter, that is something movable, relates to other such bulks.

Without further ado Hegel identifies movable bulks of matter with bodies,[168] while *body* is in fact a more specific notion. *Mechanics* moreover *presupposes* that bodies are *contiguous* in themselves, while not asking for the internal forces keeping them together. This question will rather be addressed in *Physics* which deals with matter as *in itself relational*, while *Mechanics* abstains from addressing the internal structure of material objects. On the level of *Mechanics*, bulks of matter are rather treated as if they were completely homogenous or unextended, that is as mass points.

Even while matter and motion must be essentially intertwined on a global scale, this intertwinement will leave room for independence on a subordinate scale, since nature is marked by otherness. Matter will thus be *relatively* indifferent to motion or rest.[169] That matter is indifferent, on a subordinate scale, to motion or rest means that a finite bulk of matter can as well be in motion or at rest within the same frame of reference, and whether it is one or the other will not depend on that very bulk of matter itself. From such indifference it follows that bulks of matter are inert, that is they do not change their state of motion or rest on their own initiative, but only if externally forced to do so.[170] Newton's first axiom is thus justified with regard to *finite* bulks of matter which make up a mere portion of all the matter there is in the physical universe.[171] That matter is inert if viewed on a subordinate scale does not entail that matter on the whole could as well be indifferent to motion and could thus very well be at rest. For it has already been shown that nature must involve motion, since motion is what space and time have their real unity in. Hegel thus reproaches Newton with overlooking that the law of inertia cannot apply to matter on a global scale, but is only valid with regard to finite isolated portions of all the matter there is.[172]

We already know that there *must* be motion in a spatiotemporal universe, because motion is what provides for the unity of space and time on the part of the real. There must accordingly be bulks of matter in motion. A bulk of matter, however, is as such indifferent to motion or rest. That there must be bulks of matter in motion thus raises the question for the ground of their motion. One might be inclined to respond that ultimately certain bulks of matter just *happen* to be in motion. This answer won't do, however, for all matter might then as well have happened to be at rest. Accordingly, bulks of matter cannot just happen to be in motion, but their being in motion must be due to some sort of cause. The only thing which the state of motion of a bulk of matter can be caused

---

[168] See $20,256^{10\text{-}13}$. [169] Cf. TW9, 63 A. [170] Cf. $20,256^{17\text{-}23}$. [171] Cf. $20,257^{4\text{-}8}$.
[172] Cf. $20,257^{1\text{-}4; 15\text{-}19}$.

by is matter, because matter is the only thing available for interaction. The most straightforward way in which the motion of a bulk of matter can be caused by interaction with other matter is the transmission of motion through impact.[173] Impact, however, cannot be the only way in which bulks of matter are set in motion, because this would lead to a regress insofar as it only defers the question for the ultimate ground of states of motion that can be transmitted through impact.

As it seems, we have reached an impasse, because we know that there *must* be motion, for which reason bulks of matter cannot just *happen* to be in motion, while the ultimate ground of their motion can neither be situated in themselves nor in the motion of other bulks of matter, because the latter leads to a regress, while the former contradicts the fact that bulks of matter are inert and do not accordingly set themselves in motion.

Actually, however, all that is needed to explain how matter can essentially be both, inert and in motion, is already at hand. For what is at issue is how *finite* portions of matter ultimately come by their states of motion. Ultimately they can neither *receive* their motion from other bulks of matter nor can they *set themselves in motion just on their own*, but they must rather *set themselves in motion thanks to other matter being around*. There must accordingly be a force – a way of interaction – *inherent to matter as such* in virtue of which matter sets itself in motion *in the presence of other matter which might very well be as of yet motionless* – gravity.[174] While gravity is usually conceived of as attraction of matter *by* other matter, Hegel insists that bulks of matter *strive toward* other matter rather than being attracted by it.[175] The reason for this seems to be the following: A rigid bulk of matter can only move in one direction at a time, while it will be surrounded by many other bulks of matter, given that matter is distributed throughout space. The gravitational motion of a bulk of matter will thus not be directed toward any particular bulk of matter, but toward the center of mass of different bulks of matter surrounding it. This center is not itself a bulk of matter, but an unextended and thus immaterial point.[176] Since a point, other than a thing, cannot have causal powers, heavy matter *cannot be pulled* toward a center of gravity, but it must be credited with *striving* toward it on its own initiative.

Insofar as heavy matter moves in the direction of the center of mass surrounding it, while this center isn't a real thing but an ideal unextended point, gravitational motion involves some sort of idealization on the part of matter itself, that is in nature.[177] There is accordingly a way in which a material body

---

[173] See 20,257$^{23\text{-}26}$. [174] See E§262, §§265–66. [175] See 20,255$^{14\text{-}17}$; TW9,99A.
[176] See 20,255$^{21\text{-}23}$. [177] Cf. TW9,72A.

moves toward a punctiform center of mass. Insofar as this way determines the body's motion toward an ideal point, it is itself something ideal in nature. The determinate way in which a body strives toward an ideal point that is fixed by how further matter is distributed in space, that is the law of motion, is accordingly something ideal pertaining to *nature*, rather than something merely thought.

That the lawful way in which a bulk of matter moves toward an ideal point which is the center of mass of the matter surrounding it is something ideal pertaining to nature does not mean that gravitational motion would not require something real that bridges the distance between the moving body and its ideal destination. Hegel's account of gravitational motion as an *idealization on the part of nature* is overly idealistic for the following reason: While the law of motion is the way in which a bulk of matter traverses the distance separating it from the center of mass, nature still remains the realm of externality which means that a heavy body cannot contain some sort of *inner* compass directing it toward an ideal point beyond itself. It cannot, because the space between a moving body and a distant point cannot simply be bridged by a lawful way of bridging it, but it must be bridged by something real extending through space as the modern view of the gravitational field with its gravitational waves has it.

So far, it has been implicitly assumed that gravitational motion is unilateral motion of *one* bulk of matter toward a center of mass, that is free fall. However, a center of mass is the center of mass of further matter that likewise strives toward its respective center of mass. Gravitational attraction therefore involves mutual interaction, even while the resulting motions might be unevenly distributed among the bulks of matter involved. Free fall comes first in the conceptual order of gravitational motion, according to Hegel, because it is indeed the most immediate and simple kind of gravitational motion. However, it cannot be the only kind of motion that has its source in matter as such because it is both finite and conditioned: It is finite insofar as it results in the falling body overcoming the distance separating it from further matter in which the center of mass is located. Due to its finitude, free fall, even while being self-initiated motion, is externally conditioned nonetheless: It can only occur, if the falling body finds itself at a certain distance from a center of mass which allows it to fall toward it, while it cannot, on its own initiative, put itself in a position for free fall to occur.[178]

Since motion is a *necessary* global feature of a spatiotemporal universe, a finite and conditioned kind of motion cannot be the only kind of gravitational motion there is. For neither can motion cease while space, time, and matter

---

[178] See 20,261$^{9\text{-}13}$.

prevail, nor can the *necessary* occurrence of motion be ultimately dependent on a *contingent* configuration of matter that allows bulks of matter to fall toward other matter. There must accordingly be a kind of motion that is unconditioned and potentially unending. This motion must have its source in matter's universal tendency to unite with other matter, that is in gravity. It is the task of *Absolute Mechanics* to spell out what is entailed by gravitational motion that is fully unconditioned.

2.4 *Absolute Mechanics*: Solar Systems as Manifesting the Nature of Matter

Gravity can only give rise to unconditioned potentially infinite motion, if the gravitational attraction which a bulk of matter is subject to is outbalanced by its own inertia in a way that prevents it from falling toward the center of mass of further matter. This condition can only be met, if there are bulks of matter of unequal mass which are such that one has its center in the vicinity of the other, while at the same time being sufficiently inert to not fall toward it. The unconditional, potentially infinite motion that has its source in the nature of matter will thus be orbital motion of one bulk of matter around another heavier bulk of matter.[179] In distinction to free fall this kind of motion is unconditioned insofar as it has its ground in *some sort* of uneven distribution of matter in space *or other*, rather than presupposing a *determinate unnatural* distribution of matter, namely, one in which a bulk of matter that isn't sufficiently inert to keep itself apart from the center of gravitational attraction finds itself at a distance from that center. Orbital motion is potentially infinite insofar as it involves an equilibrium between the striving of heavy matter toward other matter and the self-sufficiency that pertains to the orbiting body qua inert body.

Hegel contradicts Newton by claiming that gravitation contradicts inertia,[180] that heavenly bodies aren't subject to the law of inertia,[181] that the distinction between centripetal and centrifugal force is spurious[182] and that gravitation involves both attraction and repulsion.[183] These claims should at best be read with a grain of salt, namely, as not seeking to do away with the distinction between inertia and gravity altogether.[184] They should rather be seen as consequences of Hegel's critique of Newton's assumption that universal attraction is accidental to matter.[185] Since matter is essentially in motion, according to Hegel, matter must essentially be heavy and gravitation cannot be accidental to matter as Newton assumes. Both inertia and gravity will thus have to count as

---

[179] Cf. 20,271$^{14\text{-}17}$.   [180] See 20,266$^{17\text{-}19}$.   [181] See 20,257$^{4\text{-}11}$.   [182] See 20,266$^{21\text{-}27}$.
[183] See 20,254$^{5\text{-}13}$.
[184] On Hegel's critique of Newton's conception of gravitation cf. Houlgate 2006, 153–156.
[185] Cf. Newton 1999,796;943.

dependent aspects of the nature of matter rather than the latter amounting to an independent force additionally implanted in it.[186] On Newton's view it appears as contingent that inertia and gravity can be equilibrated in the way that gives rise to orbital motion, while such motion must rather be seen as a necessary expression of the nature of matter. The orbital motion of a celestial body cannot be understood as the result of its *accidental* deflection by other matter which *happens* to interfere with inertial motion grounded in that body's *own nature*.[187] Viewing it in this way is illegitimately assimilating infinite celestial motions to finite terrestrial motions such as impact, throw, and free fall which indeed depend on conditions which are external to matter as such.

In a certain sense Hegel thus revives the old Aristotelian distinction between terrestrial and celestial physics against Newton's leveling of it.[188] The circular motions of celestial bodies which are a consequence of the *nature* of matter need indeed to be distinguished from the motions of middle-sized bodies on celestial bodies occasioned by *accidental* pushes and pulls. Nonetheless, Hegel aligns himself with Newton against Aristotle in neither assuming that the distinction between essential and accidental motions requires us to view the Earth as the center of the universe with the heavens revolving around it nor supposing that the Earth and the heavens contain different kinds of matter which make earthly and heavenly bodies subject to different kinds of rule which would mean to fall short of the idea of universal laws of nature. Hegel goes beyond both Aristotle *and* Newton by envisaging celestial motions as the full blown expression of the nature of matter,[189] while seeing the motions of middle-sized bodies in a planetary setting as an expression of the nature of matter *if subject to accidental impact*.

By thinking through the concept of matter as something *essentially* inert *and* heavy it has been shown that the physical universe must involve bulks of matter revolving around heavier bulks of matter. We have thus arrived at the concept of a "system of multiple bulks of matter"[190] as a consequence of the concept of matter. The concept of matter revolving around a center of mass is more general than the concept of a solar system, since solar nebulae or galaxies orbiting around a common center of gravity equally instantiate it. As a philosopher of nature one might want to content oneself with proof that the revolution of matter around other matter is a consequence of its nature while leaving the study of *specific* revolutions of that sort to science. Hegel, however, seeks to go further,

---

[186] Cf. 20,254$^{5\text{-}9}$;266$^{19\text{-}21}$. According to Kluit Hegel's conception of inertia and gravity as dependent aspects of the nature of matter points beyond classical physics in which the equivalence of inertial and gravitational mass is "an accidental property of gravitation" toward general relativity in which it becomes a "necessary principle" (1993, 229).

[187] See 20,271$^{18\text{-}24}$.   [188] Cf. 20,257$^{1\text{-}19}$.   [189] Cf. 20,275$^{9\text{-}16}$.   [190] 20,266$^{5\text{-}8}$.

claiming that philosophy of nature can show that matter entails the existence of solar systems involving specific kinds of heavenly body – suns, planets, moons, and comets – which revolve in specific ways around themselves, around others or both. He also attempts to philosophically derive Kepler's laws which govern the motions of planets around the sun, detailing the elliptical shape of their orbits, the size of the areas swept out by line segments joining the planet and the sun in a certain amount of time, as well as the quantitative dependence of an orbital period on distance from the sun.[191]

There is reason to be hesitant about Hegel's ambition to philosophically derive the physical notion of a solar system as well as his attempt to deduce the laws of motion to which planets obey. Solar systems are neither global features of the physical universe nor generic kinds of motion or matter, but systems of specific material objects situated on a relatively small scale. The path from a dynamic account of matter in general to the concrete conception of a solar system is thus rather far. A philosophical attempt at showing that there is a necessary connection between matter and solar systems would have to make contact with scientific accounts of how solar systems originate, and it would have to exhibit empirical claims concerning initial conditions which such accounts rely on as in fact necessary consequences of what matter is. There is no attempt on Hegel's part to engage in this way with the then pertinent scientific theory on the issue, the Kant-Lapacian hypothesis. He rather bases his account of the solar system on the threefold division of the concept, that is the threefold logical distinction between universality, particularity, and singularity.[192] While the *Science of Logic* indeed derives the concept of a system of objects whose states are interdependent in a way that follows from the threefold division of the concept[193], the *logical* concept of *absolute mechanism* is utterly generic so as to allow all kinds of items, solar systems and political states among them, to instantiate it.[194] Hegel's ruminations on solar systems in the philosophy of nature are logicist in that he largely refrains from *further specifying* the *logical* conception of absolute mechanism so as to arrive at a *philosophical* conception of a system of material objects involving suns, planets, moons, and comets. He rather seems to render certain empirical facts about solar systems in logical terminology. For reasons that have been indicated in the first section one might be even more wary that attempting to philosophically derive mathematical laws of planetary motion is dabbling in a business that should rather be left to science.

---

[191] See 20,268^1–275^7. For a sympathetic reconstruction of Hegel's attempt to philosophically derive Kepler's laws see Houlgate 2006, 147–153.
[192] Cf. 20,267$^{14-21}$. [193] See 12,143^1–146^{23}; cf. Martin 2012, 377–387.
[194] Cf. 12,143^{16}–144^2; 12,143^{37}–145^{10}.

2.5 Hegel's *Mechanics* and Relativity Theory

One might wonder where to situate Hegel's conception of space, time, motion, and matter with regard to the classical Newtonian conception and the contemporary Einsteinian view. It has often been noted that Hegel's account has a certain affinity with relativity insofar as he rejects a view of space and time as containers which might as well be empty, viewing space and time as formal features of material processes instead. More specifically, it has been pointed out that Hegel subscribes to certain assumptions that play a role in relativity theory, both special and general. Regarding the former he has not only been said to "accept" the "Galilean principle of relativity" but to "acknowledge" that the speed of light is "absolute".[195] Regarding the latter he has been credited with subscribing to the identity of inertial and gravitational mass. In light of such findings, Stephen Houlgate argues that Hegel's philosophical account of space, time, motion and matter is "compatible" with relativity theory, stressing however, that Hegel does not reckon with matter curving space.[196] According to Houlgate, "any such distortion would have to be considered contingent from the philosophical point of view, since nothing makes it logically necessary".[197]

However, phrasing the relation between Hegel's philosophy of nature and relativity theory in terms of "compatibility" while claiming that core insights of relativity theory must count as "contingent" from a philosophical point of view, won't do. For relativity theory does not content itself with viewing quantitative correlations between space, time, mass, and motion somewhat differently from Newtonian physics. It envisages *kinds of correlation* between these global features of the physical universe which are altogether unknown to classical Mechanics: a dependence of time on velocity varying across different frames of reference, the existence of a velocity that is frame-independent, namely, the speed of light, and a dependence of space on matter, namely, its being curved by it. These dependencies, independently of how they are spelled out mathematically, concern *real* connections between *global* features of nature, and thus have a bearing on the unity of nature which is the topic of philosophy of nature. It should therefore be possible to *philosophically* account for such dependencies in a purely conceptual manner, instead of viewing them as contingent, while leaving the study of their quantitative dimension to science.

Dieter Wandschneider has argued that both axioms of special relativity – the principle of relativity and the absoluteness of the speed of light – can indeed be accounted for within the framework of Hegel's philosophy of nature,[198] which

---

[195] Houlgate 2006, 157.   [196] Houlgate 2006, 157–158.   [197] Houlgate 2006, 159.
[198] Cf. Wandschneider 1982, 189–214; Wandschneider 1987. In light of Wandschneider's investigations it is surprising, both philologically and systematically, to find Kauffman and Yeomans

allows viewing them as necessarily true rather than contingent, as they might appear from the vantage point of physics.

The *Galilean* principle of relativity according to which a body A which is in inertial motion with regard to another body B can as well count as at rest, while A counts as moving, is part of Hegel's philosophical concept of motion, as has been shown earlier. Against the background of *Mechanics* it should be possible to unpack the *Galilean* principle so as to obtain the *principle of relativity* figuring in special relativity according to which the same laws of nature apply in all inertial frames. It is the second axiom of special relativity concerning the frame-independence of the speed of light which might seem to be a contingent fact that is philosophically out of reach, even while Hegel's claim that light is "absolute velocity"[199] apparently anticipates it.

Contrary to this impression, Wandschneider has argued that Hegel's philosophy of nature contains resources that allow one to philosophically recognize the existence of an absolute speed as necessary.[200] According to Wandschneider, the concept of heavy matter, that is of bulks of matter striving toward a center of mass *outside of them* while being prevented from ever reaching their center points toward the concept of something that does *not* have its center outside of itself and is thus real but immaterial, a "non-body." Something real but immaterial would not only lack a center outside of itself toward which it strives but it would also not be inert. Not being inert, it would either have to be essentially at rest or essentially in motion. The former possibility is ruled out, however, because an A that is supposed to be essentially at rest would still have to count as being in motion from the vantage point of a B that is in motion from the vantage point of A. Something real but immaterial is therefore *essentially* in motion. Insofar as it is essentially in motion, its motion cannot be frame-dependent, because otherwise there would inevitably be a frame with regard to which it is at rest.

This line of argument is compelling, but only as a *hypothetical*: *If* there is something real but immaterial which is as such necessarily in motion, its velocity cannot be relative but must rather be absolute, being the same with regard to all inertial frames. However, even while something real but immaterial would have to move frame-independently and have absolute velocity, relying on a merely reflective contrast between the material and the immaterial, Wandschneider's argument does not show why something of this sort, namely, light, must actually exist. It does not show that the absolute motion of a kind of

---

claim that the "all important feature" of relativity theory "that a precise ratio of time and space, the speed of light, is preserved" is "of course, outside of Hegel's context" (2023, 101). For an Anglophone appreciation of Wandschneider's results cf. Houlgate 2006, 156–160.

[199] TW9, 112A.   [200] Cf. Wandschneider 1987, 306–307.

"non-body" is a necessary feature of nature without which the spatiotemporal universe would essentially lack unity.

To philosophically make good on Hegel's claim that there must be something in nature that is essentially in motion and whose speed is thus absolute, one might argue as follows: The relation between space and time must be real, rather than merely thought. Since nature is quantitatively determined, the real dependence between space and time must involve a variation of one depending on variation of the other. Time cannot *directly* vary with space,[201] while spatial position can directly vary with time. This variation, motion, is thus a necessary feature of the spatiotemporal universe. However, the real unity between space and time must go both ways. There must thus be an *indirect* way in which time depends on space, rather than being altogether independent of it. For there to be a real unity between space and time which goes both ways, even while not varying *directly* with space, time must vary indirectly with it by way of varying with a physical magnitude which, in turn, depends on space, namely, motion, or, more concretely, velocity. The passage of time, however, cannot depend on velocity *in an immediate manner*, namely, *in one and the same frame of reference*, because motion involves a quantitative variation of space with time: $\delta s(\delta t)$. *One and the same* variable cannot be both an independent and a dependent one: If a change of place δs depends on the passage of time δt, δt cannot in turn depend on the speed $\delta s/\delta t$, because independently of the anterior fixation of δt this speed would not have a determinate value.

We can conclude: Since the passage of time must vary with velocity, while it cannot directly do so within one frame of reference, it must vary across different frames of reference which are in motion with regard to one another. There must accordingly be events which occur within one such system at the same time, while occurring from the vantage point of the other system at different times.

As quantitative relations, simultaneity and non-simultaneity are only determined with regard to something that provides a measure, that is a clock. Apparently, the simultaneity and non-simultaneity of events occurring in different places A and C is *simply* determined by whether these events occur exactly when a clock in an arbitrary place B indicates a certain time. However, this view of simultaneity is imaginary in that it overlooks that the relations between events in places A and C to the clock in B must be real, rather than merely thought or imagined. Simultaneity or non-simultaneity in different places will thus only be determined by way of a real process that links these events to a clock. The problem of establishing simultaneity and non-simultaneity with regard to different places cannot be resolved by first

---

[201] Cf. fn. 141.

synchronizing two clocks in the same place and then bringing one of them to another place. For it has already been established that the passage of time depends on the state of motion of the reference frame. Bringing one clock to another place, while leaving the other where it is, would therefore lead to desynchronization.

Simultaneity in different places can therefore only be established on the basis of signals which travel the same distance in the same time. Clocks in different places A and C can thus be synchronized by way of sending signals which are known to have the same speed toward points A and C which are equidistant from point B in which the signals start. Such signals, however, cannot be material for the following reason. The motion of matter is subject to the principle of relativity which entails in this case that signals which arrive at their destinations A and C simultaneously from the vantage point of one frame of reference will arrive simultaneously as well from the vantage point of any other frame of reference with regard to which the former frame of reference is in (inertial) motion.

Knowing both that simultaneity in different places can only be established by way of signals, and that simultaneity must be frame-dependent, while material signals cannot establish frame-dependence, we can conclude that there must be something with an absolute, frame-independent velocity. For it is only thanks to the existence of a sort of signal that moves with the same velocity in all frames of reference that simultaneity is determined in a way that makes it depend on the state of motion of the reference frame.

By way of purely conceptual considerations we have thus established that there must be something that moves with absolute speed, that is independently of the frame of reference, that is light. For given that it has been shown that time and, more concretely, simultaneity must depend on motion and must thus vary across reference frames which are in motion in relation to one another, we can conclude that there must be a kind of motion that establishes simultaneity in a frame-dependent way, that is a signal which has absolute velocity. What has absolute velocity is not inert and, thus, immaterial.[202] We have thus derived the necessary existence of something immaterial *in nature* whose speed is absolute, that is light, and we have thus made good on Hegel's conception of light as "absolute velocity."

While the absoluteness of the speed of light has an axiomatic character in the special theory of relativity and is based on empirical evidence, the philosophical argument just sketched establishes that there must be something real whose

---

[202] On Hegel's conception of immateriality and the role of the immaterial in his system cf. Wretzel 2021.

speed is absolute. While Einstein proceeds from the empirical fact that the speed of light is absolute and, based on this, shows that simultaneity is frame-dependent,[203] we have shown, by way of philosophical argument, that time and, hence, simultaneity must be frame-dependent, while concluding from this that there must be something whose speed is absolute, namely, light, because it is only on condition of the existence of signals with absolute speed that simultaneity can be frame-dependent. If this reasoning is conclusive, it shows that matter and light belong together necessarily, rather than contingently, and that there must be a quantity in nature which is constant, namely, the speed of light.[204]

---

[203] See Einstein 1905.

[204] Due to rigid external constraints set by the publisher this Element ends here. This makes it a fragmented, rather than a comprehensive treatment of Hegel's philosophy of nature. I had in fact written and wished to include a third chapter dealing with the remaining parts of Hegel's philosophy of nature. For better or worse, instead of being contained in this volume, this text, entitled "Physics and Organic Physics: from States of Matter to Life on Earth," is available on my academia, philpapers, and University of Stuttgart webpages.

Abbreviations

A.	Addition [in TW]
AA	Kant, *Gesammelte Schriften*
CPR	*Critique of Pure Reason*
E	*Encyclopedia of the Philosophical Sciences* (1830)
SW	Schelling, *Sämmtliche Werke*
TW	Hegel, *Werke*

Hegel's *Gesammelte Werke* are quoted according to the following schema: volume, page$^{\text{line(s)}}$. $12,23^{3\text{-}6}$, for instance, refers to volume 12, page 23, lines 3–6.

References

Aristotle. 1933. *Metaphysics. Books 1–9.* (Loeb Classical Library No. 271). Cambridge, MA: Harvard University Press.

Aristotle. 1957. *De anima.* (Loeb Classical Library No. 288). Cambridge, MA: Harvard University Press.

Aristotle. 1957. *The Physics. Books 1–4.* (Loeb Classical Library No. 228). Cambridge, MA: Harvard University Press.

Barrow, J. 2001. *The Book of Nothing.* London: Vintage Books.

Berger, B. 2023. *Schelling, Hegel, and the Philosophy of Nature: From Matter to Spirit.* London: Routledge.

Bonsiepen, W. 1997. *Die Begründung einer Naturphilosophie bei Kant, Schelling, Fries und Hegel.* Frankfurt: Klostermann.

Collingwood, F. 1973. Comment on Findlay's "Hegel and the Philosophy of Physics." In J. J. O'Malley, K. W. Algozin, H. P. Kainz and L. C. Rice (eds.) *The Legacy of Hegel.* The Hague: Martinus Nijhoff, pp. 90–97.

Corti, L. and Schülein, J.-G. (eds.) 2022. *Nature and Naturalism in Classical German Philosophy.* London: Routledge.

Corti, L. and Schülein, J.-G. (eds.) 2023. *Life, Organisms, and Human Nature: New Perspectives on Classical German Philosophy.* Cham: Springer Nature.

Davies, P. 1986. *The Forces of Nature.* Cambridge: Cambridge University Press.

Einstein, A. 1905. Zur Elektrodynamik bewegter Körper. *Annalen der Physik* 322 (10), pp. 891–920.

Engelhardt, D. von. 1976. *Hegel und die Chemie: Studie zur Philosophie und Wissenschaft der Natur um 1800.* Wiesbaden: Pressler.

Falcon, A. 2005. *Aristotle and the Science of Nature: Unity without Uniformity.* Cambridge: Cambridge University Press.

Ferrarin, A. 1998. *Aristotelian and Newtonian Models in Hegel's Philosophy of Nature.* In R. S. Cohen and A. I. Tauber (eds.) *Philosophies of Nature: The Human Dimension.* Dordrecht: Kluwer Academic, pp. 71–89.

Ferrer, D. and Krijnen, C. (eds.) 2025. *Hegelian Perspectives on the Philosophy of Nature and the Environment.* Leiden: Brill.

Ferrini, C. 2014. From Disparagement to Appreciation: Shifting Paradigms and Interdisciplinary Openings in Interpreting Hegel's Philosophy of Nature. *Esercizi Filosofici* 9 (1), pp. 1–13.

Findlay, J. 1973. Hegel and the Philosophy of Physics. In J. J. O'Malley, K. W. Algozin, H. P. Kainz and L. C. Rice (eds.) *The Legacy of Hegel.* The Hague: Martinus Nijhoff, pp. 72–89.

Förster, E. 2012. *The Twenty-Five Years of Philosophy: A Systematic Reconstruction*. Cambridge, MA: Harvard University Press.

Förster, E. 2022. Kants Materietheorie im Lichte der Kritik Schellings. In J. Haag and B. Beyer (eds.) *Grenzen der Erkenntnis?* Stuttgart-Bad Cannstatt: Frommann-Holzboog, pp. 171–192.

Friedman, M. 2007. Kant – Naturphilosophie – Electromagnetism. In R. M. Brain, R. S. Cohen and O. Knudsen (eds.) *Hans Christian Ørsted and the Romantic Legacy in Science*. Heidelberg: Springer, pp. 135–158.

Fulda, H. F. 2003. *Georg Wilhelm Friedrich Hegel*. München: Beck.

Haase, M. 2013. Life and Mind. In T. Khurana (ed.) *The Freedom of Life: Hegelian Perspectives*. Berlin: August Verlag, pp. 69–110.

Hadot, P. 2004. *Le voile d'Isis. Essai sur l'histoire de l'idée de la Nature*. Paris: Gallimard.

Hegel, G. W. F. 1968–2020. *Gesammelte Werke*. Hamburg: Meiner.

Hegel, G. W. F. 1970. *Werke in 20 Bänden*. Frankfurt: Suhrkamp.

Hegel, G. W. F. 1970. *The Philosophy of Nature*. 3 Vols. Trans. J. M. Petry. London: George Allen and Unwin.

Hegel, G. W. F. 2010. *The Science of Logic*. Trans. G. di Giovanni. Cambridge: Cambridge University Press.

Hendry, R. F. 2010. Ontological Reduction and Molecular Structure. *Studies in History and Philosophy of Modern Physics* 41, pp. 183–191.

Hertz, H. 1899. *The Principles of Mechanics Presented in a New Form*. London: Macmillan.

Hösle, V. 1998. *Hegels System Der Idealismus der Subjektivität und das Problem der Intersubjektivität*. Hamburg: Meiner.

Houlgate, S. 2005. *An Introduction to Hegel: Freedom, Truth and History*. 2nd ed. London: Blackwell.

Houlgate, S. 2006. *The Opening of Hegel's Logic: From Being to Infinity*. West Lafayette: Purdue University Press.

Houlgate, S. 2024. Logic and Physics in Hegel's Philosophy of Nature. In M. Bykova (ed.) *Hegel's Philosophy of Nature: A Critical Guide*. Cambridge: Cambridge University Press, pp. 176–198.

Illetterati, L. 2024. *Realität als Äußerlichkeit: Für eine unitarische Lektüre von Hegels Realphilosophie*. In H. Plevrakis (ed.) *Hegels Philosophie der Realität*. Leiden: Brill, pp. 214–233.

Jacobson, M., Charlson, H. and Orians, G. H. 2000. *Earth System Science: From Biogeochemical Cycles to Global Change*. Amsterdam: Elsevier.

Kant, I. 1900ff. *Gesammelte Schriften*. Berlin: Georg Reimer et al.

Kant, I. 1929. *Critique of Pure Reason*. Trans. N. Kemp Smith. London: Macmillan.

Kant, I. 1990. *Kritik der reinen Vernunft*. Hamburg: Meiner.

Kauffman, R. and Yeomans, C. 2023. Hegel's Theory of Space-Time (No, Not That Space-Time). In L. Corti and J.-G. Schülein (eds.) *Life, Organisms, and Human Nature: New Perspectives on Classical German Philosophy*. Cham: Springer Nature, pp. 97–120.

Kluit, P. M. 1993. Inertial and Gravitational Mass: Newton, Hegel, and Modern Physics. In J. M. Petry (ed.) *Hegel and Newtonianism*. Dordrecht: Kluwer Academic, pp. 229–247.

Koch, A. 2014. *Die Evolution des logischen Raumes*. Tübingen: Mohr Siebeck.

Koschel, M. 2025. The Freedom of Solar Systems. *Hegel Bulletin* 43 (1), pp. 100–129.

Kosman, A. 2013. *The Activity of Being: An Essay on Aristotle's Ontology*. Cambridge, MA: Harvard University Press.

Kreines, J. 2015. *Reason in the World: Hegel's Metaphysics and its Philosophical Appeal*. Oxford: Oxford University Press.

Lepenies, W. 1978. *Das Ende der Naturgeschichte: Wandel kultureller Selbstverständlichkeiten in den Wissenschaften des 18. und 19. Jahrhunderts*. Frankfurt: Suhrkamp.

Lyssy, A. 2024. A Past without History and the Conditions of Life: Hegel on the Terrestrial Organism. In M. Bykova (ed.) *Hegel's Philosophy of Nature. A Critical Guide*. Cambridge: Cambridge University Press, pp. 217–237.

Magee, A. G. 2001. *Hegel and the Hermetic Tradition*. Ithaca: Cornell University Press.

Maker, W. 1998. The Very Idea of the Idea of Nature, or Why Hegel Is Not an Idealist. In S. Houlgate (ed.) *Hegel's Philosophy of Nature*. New York: SUNY Press, pp. 1–27.

Marmasse, G. 2008. *Penser le réel: Hegel, la nature et l'esprit*. Paris: Editions Kimé.

Marmasse, G. 2025. *Spekulation als konkrete Verallgemeinerung endlichen Wissens. Der Fall der Naturwissenschaften*. In D. Emundts and K. Koch and Quadflieg (eds.) *Das Selbstverständnis der Philosophie und ihr Verhältnis zu den (anderen) Wissenschaften*. Hamburg: Meiner, pp. 387–400.

Martin, C. 2011. Zur Logik des Lebensbegriffs. In P. Dabrock, M. Bölker, M. Braun, J. Ried (eds.) *Was ist Leben im Zeitalter seiner technischen Machbarkeit?* Freiburg: Alber, pp. 117–146.

Martin, C. 2012. *Ontologie der Selbstbestimmung: Eine operationale Rekonstruktion von Hegels, Wissenschaft der Logik'*. Tübingen: Mohr Siebeck.

Martin, C. 2020a. *Die Einheit des Sinns: Untersuchungen zur Form des Denkens und Sprechens*. Paderborn: Brill|Mentis.

Martin, C. 2020b. Kant on Concepts, Intuitions, and the Continuity of Space. *Idealistic Studies* 50 (3), pp. 233–259.

Martin, C. 2021. From Logic to Nature. In S. Stein and J. Wretzel (eds.) *Hegel's Encyclopedia of the Philosophical Sciences: A Critical Guide*. Cambridge: Cambridge University Press, pp. 88–108.

Martin, C. 2022. Three Attitudes towards Nature. *Hegel Bulletin* 43 (1), pp. 1–25.

Martin, C. 2024. *Die Erde als realer Ort des Geistes*. In H. Plevrakis (ed.) *Hegels Philosophie der Realität*. Leiden: Brill, pp. 235–251.

Martin, C. 2025a. *Die Erdgebundenheit des Lebens als philosophisches Problem*. In K. Ott and G. Oswald (eds.) *Das Leben im Fokus*, pp. 19–44.

Martin, C. 2025b. *Pure Thought of Nature*. In F. Ganzinger and C. Martin (eds.) *The Concept of Nature in Kant, Schelling, and Hegel*. Berlin: de Gruyter, Forthcoming.

Martin, C. 2025c. *Late Schelling on the Natural Origins of the Universe*. In F. Ganzinger and C. Martin (eds.) *The Concept of Nature in Kant, Schelling, and Hegel*. Berlin: de Gruyter, Forthcoming.

Martin, C. 2025d. *Hegel on the Four Elements as a Precondition of Life*. In D. Ferrer and C. Krijnen (eds.) *Hegelian Perspectives on the Philosophy of Nature and the Environment*. Leiden/Boston: Brill, Forthcoming.

McDowell, J. 1996. *Mind and World*. Cambridge, MA: Harvard University Press.

Mittelstrass, J. 1981. Das Wirken der Natur: Materialien zur Geschichte des Naturbegriffs. In F. Rapp (ed.) *Naturverständnis und Naturbeherrschung: Philosophiegeschichtliche Entwicklung und gegenwärtiger Kontext*. München: Fink, pp. 36–69.

Newton, I. 1999. *The Principia: Mathematical Principles of Natural Philosophy*. Trans. I. B. Cohen. Berkeley: University of California Press.

Ng, K. 2020. *Hegel's Concept of Life: Self-Consciousness, Freedom, Logic*. Oxford: Oxford University Press.

Olvera, Z. and Reyes, J. A. 2021. Hegel: la vida de la idea & el des-encerrarse hacia la Naturaleza. In J. Balladares, Y. Elguera, F. Huesca and Z. Olvera (eds.) *Hegel. Actualidad de su Lógica y su Sistema*. Lima: Ande, pp. 103-130.

Petry, J. M. (ed.) 1987. *Hegel und die Naturwissenschaften*. Stuttgart-Bad Cannstatt: Frommann-Holzboog.

Petry, J. M. (ed.) 1993. *Hegel and Newtonianism*. Dordrecht: Kluwer Academic.

Pinkard, T. 2004. Speculative Naturphilosophie and the Development of Empirical Sciences: Hegel's Perspective. In G. Gutting (ed.), *Continental Philosophy of Science*. London: Blackwell, pp. 17–34.

Pippin, R. 2018. *Hegel's Realm of Shadows: Logic as Metaphysics in "The Science of Logic."* Chicago: University of Chicago Press.

Prauss, G. 2017. *Das Kontinuum und das Unendliche: nach Aristoteles und Kant ein Rätsel*. Freiburg: Alber.

Rand, S. 2007. The Importance and Relevance of Hegel's Philosophy of Nature. *The Review of Metaphysics* 61, pp. 379–400.

Rand, S. 2017. Hegel's Philosophy of Nature. In D. Moyar (ed.) *The Oxford Handbook of Hegel*. Oxford: Oxford University Press, pp. 384–406.

Redding, P. 2021. Actualist versus Naturalist and Conceptual Realist Interpretations of Hegel's Metaphysics. *Hegel Bulletin* 42, pp. 19–38.

Schambaugh, C. 2025. Hegels Philosophy of Sound. *Hegel Bulletin* 46 (1), pp. 1–24. https://doi.org/10.1017/hgl.2023.19.

Schelling, F. W. J. 1856–1861. *Sämmtliche Werke*. Stuttgart und Augsburg: J. G. Cotta.

Sell, A. 2014. *Der lebendige Begriff. Leben und Logik bei G. W. F. Hegel*. Freiburg: Alber.

Spaemann, R. 1972. *Natur*. In H. Krings (ed.) *Handbuch philosophischer Grundbegriffe. Band 3*. München: Kösel, pp. 956–969.

Spahn, C. 2007. *Lebendiger Begriff, begriffenes Leben. Zur Grundlegung der Philosophie des Organischen bei G. W. F. Hegel*. Würzburg: Königshausen und Neumann.

Stein, S. 2024. Nature and Its Limits: Hegel's Idealist Critiques of Physicalism, Naturalism, and Essentialism. In M. Bykova (ed.) *Hegel's Philosophy of Nature: A Critical Guide*. Cambridge: Cambridge University Press, pp. 36–57.

Stekeler-Weithofer, P. 2001. Hegels Naturphilosophie.: Versuch einer topischen Bestimmung. *Hegel-Studien* 36, pp. 117–145.

Stekeler, P. 2023. *Hegels Realphilosophie: Ein dialogischer Kommentar zur Idee der Natur un ddes Geistes in der »Enzyklopädie der philosophischen Wissenschaften«*. Hamburg: Meiner.

Stone, A. 2005. *Petrified Intelligence: Nature in Hegel's Philosophy*. Ithaca: State University of New York Press.

Stern, R. 2018. Kreines on the Problem of Metaphysics in Kant and Hegel. *Hegel Bulletin* 39, pp. 106–120.

Stichweh, R. 1984. *Zur Entstehung des modernen Systems wissenschaftlicher Disziplinen: Physik in Deutschland 1740–1890*. Frankfurt: Suhrkamp.

Stone, A. 2005. *Petrified Intelligence: Nature in Hegel's Philosophy*. Ithaca: State University of New York Press.

Vieyra, A. 2025. Philosophical Interest and Objective Teleology in Hegel. In F. Ganzinger and C. Martin (eds.) *The Concept of Nature in Kant, Schelling, and Hegel*. Berlin: de Gruyter, Forthcoming.

Wandschneider, D. 1982. *Raum, Zeit, Relativität: Grundbestimmungen der Physik in der Perspektive der Hegelschen Naturphilosophie*. Frankfurt: Klostermann.

Wandschneider, D. 1986. Relative und absolute Bewegung in der Relativitätstheorie und in der Deutung Hegels. In R.-P. Horstmann and J. M. Petry (eds.), *Hegels Philosophie der Natur.* Stuttgart: Klett Cotta, pp. 350–362.

Wandschneider, D. 1987. Die Kategorien Materie und Licht in der Naturphilosophie Hegels. In J. M. Petry (ed.) *Hegel und die Naturwissenschaften.* Stuttgart-Bad Cannstatt: Frommann-Holzboog, pp. 293–322.

Warren, D. 2010. Kant on Attractive and Repulsive Force: The Balancing Argument. In M. Friedman, M. Domsky and M. Dickson (eds.) *Discourse on a New Method: Reinvigorating the Marriage of History and Philosophy of Science.* Chicago: Open Court, pp. 193–241.

Wieland, W. 1992. *Die Aristotelische Physik.* Göttingen: Vandenhoeck & Rupprecht.

Winfield. R. D. 2017. *Conceiving Nature after Aristotle, Kant, and Hegel: The Philosopher's Guide to the Universe.* Camden: Palgrave Macmillan.

Winfield, R. D. 2018. *Universal Biology after Aristotle, Kant, and Hegel: The Philosopher's Guide to Life in the Universe.* Camden: Palgrave Macmillan.

Wretzel, J. I. 2021. Hegel's Critique of Materialism. In S. Stein and J. Wretzel (eds.) *Hegel's Encyclopedia of the Philosophical Sciences: A Critical Guide.* Cambridge: Cambridge University Press, pp. 148–165.

Cambridge Elements

The Philosophy of Georg Wilhelm Friedrich Hegel

Sebastian Stein
Heidelberg University

Sebastian Stein is a Research Associate at Heidelberg University. He is co-editor of *Hegel's Political Philosophy* (2017), *Hegel and Contemporary Practical Philosophy* (with James Gledhill, 2019) and *Hegel's Encyclopedic System* (2021), and has authored several journal articles and chapters on Aristotle, Kant, post-Kantian idealism and (neo-)naturalism.

Joshua Wretzel
Pennsylvania State University

Joshua Wretzel is Assistant Teaching Professor of Philosophy at the Pennsylvania State University. He is the co-editor of *Hegel's Encyclopedic System* and *Hegel's Encyclopedia of the Philosophical Sciences: A Critical Guide* (Cambridge). His articles on Hegel and the German philosophical tradition have appeared in multiple edited collections and peer-reviewed journals, including the *European Journal of Philosophy* and *International Journal for Philosophical Studies*.

About the Series
These Elements provide insights into all aspects of Hegel's thought and its relationship to philosophical currents before, during, and after his time. They offer fresh perspectives on well-established topics in Hegel studies, and in some cases use Hegelian categories to define new research programs and to complement existing discussions.

Cambridge Elements

The Philosophy of Georg Wilhelm Friedrich Hegel

Elements in the Series

Hegel and Heidegger on Time
Ioannis Trisokkas

Hegel and Colonialism
Daniel James and Franz Knappik

Hegel's Sublation of Transcendental Idealism
Christian Krijnen

Hegel on the Family Form
Andreja Novakovic

Hegel's Philosophy of Nature
Christian Martin

A full series listing is available at: www.cambridge.org/EPGH

Printed by Integrated Books International,
United States of America